SUMMA PUBLICATIONS, INC.

Thomas M. Hines
Publisher

William C. Carter
Editor-in-chief

Editorial Board

Benjamin F. Bart
University of Pittsburgh

William Berg
University of Wisconsin

Germaine Brée
Wake Forest University

Michael Cartwright
McGill University

Hugh M. Davidson
University of Virginia

John D. Erickson
Louisiana State University

Wallace Fowlie
Duke University
(emeritus)

James Hamilton
University of Cincinnati

Freeman G. Henry
University of South Carolina

Grant E. Kaiser
Emory University

Norris J. Lacy
University of Kansas

Edouard Morot-Sir
University of North Carolina, Chapel Hill
(emeritus)

Jerry C. Nash
University of New Orleans

Albert Sonnenfeld
University of Southern California

Ronald W. Tobin
University of California, Santa Barbara

Philip A. Wadsworth
University of South Carolina
(emeritus)

Orders:
Box 20725
Birmingham, AL 35216

Editorial Address:
3601 Westbury Road
Birmingham, AL 35223

SOCRATIC SATIRE

SOCRATIC SATIRE

An Essay on Diderot and *Le Neveu de Rameau*

by

Stephen Werner

SUMMA PUBLICATIONS, INC.
Birmingham, Alabama
1987

Copyright 1987
Summa Publications, Inc.

ISBN 0-917786-59-9
Library of Congress Catalog Number 87-62171

Printed in the United States of America

For Karen

Acknowledgements

This study has benefited from the collegiality I have enjoyed over the years with Patrick Coleman and the stimulation of teaching courses on eighteenth-century French literature at UCLA. It owes much to the patience and determination of Susan Delaney, my Research Assistant. Geoffrey Strickland read earlier versions of the text and was an unfailing source of encouragement.

S. W.

CONTENTS

I.	Introduction: Diderot and Satire	1
II.	Horatian Satire	7
III.	*L'homme orchestre*	23
IV.	Anti-Theater	39
V.	*Satyre 2de*	55
VI.	Conclusion: From Satire to Irony	69
	Notes	75
	Bibliography	101

I

Introduction

Diderot and Satire

SATIRE IS THE MAJOR LITERARY FORM of Diderot's *œuvre* and the key to its unity of design.¹ Satire governs the mix of "literature and philosophy" found in all of Diderot's stories as a matter of course.² Its presence fosters the parody of genres and styles, plays of self-conscious narration and "deconstruction" which are signature motifs for any Diderot text. Above all, satire is inseparable from a highly unorthodox view held by Diderot about the nature of comic writing. It is that comedy is not, as Voltaire and other *philosophes* held it to be, a minor literary interest, akin to a *facétie* or entertainment.³ Comedy, and the ironies to which it gives rise, is a deeply creative Socratic⁴ mode: the source of the modernity which Diderot, more than any other *philosophe,* helped invent and bring into being.⁵ In an aesthetic of satire lies the originality of Diderot, and the reason for his standing as the eighteenth-century writer whose stories are richest in implications for contemporary readings of *philosophe* fiction and the meaning of the Enlightenment.

The genres in which this view is worked out are numerous. They reflect Diderot's love for odd, or as he was to put it in *Le Rêve de d'Alembert,* "chèvre-pied" forms,⁶ as well as a curious tendency of the eighteenth century. It is to structure the more celebrated literary fictions of the time in narratives that do not fit into clear categories or genres.⁷

Diderot's best-known works, for example, apply satiric procedures to the novel and achieve unexpected effects of parody and ironic creation. *Les Bijoux Indiscrets,* Diderot's first venture into the field, performs a take-off on Crébillon fils and the *roman galant* through the novel discourse (and narrative style) of the talking jewels.[8] *La Religieuse* pulls the rug out from under the sentimental novel and Richardson by means of the *Préface-Annexe*. The latter is a second story embedded in the text. Its ironies and comic mystifications undercut the sobriety of the tale of Suzanne Simonin and challenge its legitimacy as a tragic *mémoire*.[9] Similar interests sustain *Jacques le fataliste,* Diderot's greatest novel and a key aesthetic writing of the eighteenth century. This text draws a critical arabesque on *Tristram Shandy* and a tradition of the anti-novel that harks back to *Don Quixote*. Through the central image of *le grand rouleau,* or great scroll of fate, the story also stands as an inquiry into the meaning of literature and aesthetic representation.[10]

In narratives where a philosophical or discursive side takes precedence over storytelling, it is philosophy, in the leisurely eighteenth-century sense of the term, that comes in for reassessment. *Le Supplément au voyage de Bougainville* brings the *conte philosophique* up to date through *emboîtements* like that of Polly Baker and highly unusual subjects like sexuality and population.[11] *La Lettre sur les aveugles* turns an inquiry on blindness into a philosophical playlet whose last pages show Saunderson, the English philosopher and sage whose natural morality provides the dramatic pulse of the tale, undergoing a deathbed illumination worthy of the best pages in Voltaire.[12] *Le Rêve de d'Alembert* displays a similar mood of comic invention. The work is a kind of critical farce. It shows d'Alembert, France's greatest eighteenth-century mathematician and, along with Diderot, chief encyclopedist, undergoing an initiation into a new science of materialism: mumbling incoherent phrases about experiments in "digesting marble," babbling like a baby in his night sheets, and, in general, sowing the seeds of a visionary poetry which goes back to Lucretius.[13]

Satire's presence may be found too in many small texts which dot the Diderot landscape. *Ceci n'est pas un conte* develops an ostensible *historiette* into a narrative as demanding as many a page in *Jacques le fataliste*.[14] *L'Essai sur les règnes de Claude et de Néron* turns a book review on the life of one of Diderot's favored classical ancestors into a story of an autobiographical kind (a technique found in *La Réfutation d'Helvétius* as well).[15] Even *Les Regrets sur ma vieille robe de chambre* follows this pattern of satiric invention. Though the work is an essay, and a brief one at that, its shadings and plays of irony give it a depth not unlike that found in the writings of de Quincey or Baudelaire. And the discussion of problems of art and painting found in the essay relates it to a style later to find favor in the *Salons*.[16]

It is in *Le Neveu de Rameau,* a writing generally considered to be Diderot's masterpiece, if not indeed "a paradigm of the modern cultural and spiritual situation,"[17] that these comic procedures are applied to an even more problematical (and potentially significant) literary form. This form is satire. Satire's presence is underscored in three parts of the work. They are the title, *Le Neveu de Rameau ou Satyre 2de;* the main character called Lui, a ne'er-do-well bohemian musician and nephew of the great French opera composer and musical theorist Jean-François Rameau; and the story's form. The latter elevates the mixture of genres and styles fundamental to satire to a blend of dialogue and theater, music and pantomime unknown in any previous *philosophe* writing.[18]

Satire could not be more elusive in nature. On the one hand, the term refers to a specific literary form or tradition. It is, as Frye has written, the Latin one exploited by Horace and Juvenal in verse; and the prose or "menippean satire" developed by writers like Lucian and Petronius.[19] On the other hand, satire escapes genre. It is a free-floating mode. For the contrasts between the real and the ideal, the poetic and the prosaic, cannot be fenced off in a single form, however complex. Such dualities are encountered in other types of aesthetic expression as well. Among them are the prints of Goya and Hogarth, and, in music, the self-parody implicit in Liszt's transcriptions of Wagner.

Nor with the choice of satire can it be said that Diderot has given in to the confusion which readers of a not too distant past thought of as emblematic of his world. Diderot, it was said, was a writer whose head and heart rode in separate harness and whose outlook could best be compared to a weather vane spinning this way and that with each change of the wind, never settling on any one spot unless it be variability.[20]

The satiric reference allows Diderot to deepen the critical properties of his art and to define in an even more radical way its modernity of intent. The form of satire encourages these interests, to be sure. For satire is, as Roger Zuber has stated, the most protean of literary genres:

> ...la satire est une des formes les plus difficiles à cerner. Où la tragédie et la comédie, voire le roman, offrent l'appui, même incertain, d'une formule consacrée, et semblent occuper un domaine délimité, la satire menace de s'insinuer partout, au théâtre, dans la prose et dans l'épopée, comme à travers les strophes lyriques les plus diverses. Cet "esprit satirique", aussi vague qu'insistant, outre qu'il suscite l'émotion moqueuse du destinataire, traduit, chez l'auteur, une révolte, disons mieux: le refus d'être complice.[21]

As such, it encourages the highly unusual mixtures of forms, styles and "carnival" interests central to Diderot's world. By carnival is meant a work organized as a survey or encyclopedia of the genre in which it was written (the novel, or anti-novel, in *Jacques le fataliste,* for example, or *le conte philosophique* in *Le Supplément au voyage de Bougainville* and *Le Rêve de d'Alembert*).

Even more crucial to an understanding of Diderot's view of satire is the status of the form in the eighteenth century. It is as an exemplary literary genre. Satire embodies key *philosophe* interests in didactic fiction and comic writing. As Lanson has written in his still highly readable *L'Art de la prose,* one can call it a *forme fixe.* Satire sums up the mood of the period that has come to be known as the Enlightenment:

> Le XVIIe siècle s'était donné la "maxime" et le "portrait" pour couler ses observations morales. Le XVIIIe siècle, pour "illustrer" la critique universelle des idées et des institutions, organisa l' "apologue" et l' "allégorie", le "conte", le "dialogue", et ces fantaisies indéfinissables que l'on ramasse sous le nom de "facétie". Ces sortes d'écrits sont exactement des formes fixes: elles s'offrent à quiconque veut présenter aux gens du monde une idée abstraite ou un ensemble d'idées. L' "allégorie", l' "apologue", sont des métaphores ou des comparaisons développées; le "conte", le "dialogue", la "facétie", sont des cadres disposés pour recevoir les petits faits concrets, les détails pittoresques et vivants qui peuvent réaliser la pensée philosophique.[22]

The reader of *Le Neveu de Rameau* is tipped off, as is frequently the case in Diderot, to the narrator's interest in challenging this exemplary view of satire. The reference occurs in a seemingly innocuous part of the story which, following a tradition of ironic subversion from within, turns out to be rich in associations of a critical kind. The subtitle of *Le Neveu de Rameau* serves this function. It reads: *Satyre 2de*.

"Second Satire" is, one might well expect, a mystification. Diderot's *œuvre* contains two writings which are entitled satires. One is *Rameau's Nephew*. The other is a short work in the style of a rambling journal influenced by Montaigne: *Satire Première, Sur les caractères et les mots de caractère, de profession, etc. Satyre 2de*, though—*Rameau's Nephew*—was written before *Satire Première*. It has a more legitimate claim to the title *First Satire* than the writing which actually bears the name.[23]

Yet for all its ambiguity, *Second Satire* is no less fundamental to an understanding of *Le Neveu de Rameau*. The phrase highlights the hidden project of Diderot's text. This project is the modernization of satire. Diderot's spelling of satire provides the clue to this interest. It rejects the normal usage of "satire," found in editions of Boileau or Voltaire contemporary with Diderot, in favor of *satyre*. The latter is an anachronism or throwback to an earlier form.

As Riffaterre has observed, anachronisms are not always quaint or archaic. They can also express qualities of critical contrast and transgression. Anachronisms violate the authority of known traditions and norms.[24] They convey the power of creative invention. The "y" of *satyre* points to this state. It is not the traditional Latin or neoclassical spelling but a Greek one (specifically identified as a variant in the *Encyclopédie* article devoted to satire). As such *satyre* emphasizes an early, even primitive, version of the genre. It is the one whose authority Diderot's narrator hopes to capture in his second or modern rendering.

This essay is a study of Diderot's *Second Satire*. Two assumptions guide the arguments advanced within. The first is that Diderot did indeed change the face of satire in *Le Neveu de Rameau*. He removed satire from its traditional status as a mild comic entertainment or *facétie* and made it into a major literary form whose complexities of narration (and depth of psychology) ally it with the novel. The second assumption is that Italian opera—*opera buffa*—is the vehicle for this metamorphosis. Opera is portrayed in Diderot's story as a Socratic art form. It possesses the disseminative force and power for change characteristic of all authentic idioms of this kind.

Reading a Socratic work will not be easy. Study of many patterns of ironic displacement and mystification will be called for, as well as an understanding of various crossovers between literature and other arts. It is to an effort at uncovering these patterns and at relating them to the aesthetics of Diderot and the Enlightenment that the following chapters are devoted.[25]

II

Horatian Satire

LE NEVEU DE RAMEAU OPENS with an epigraph from Horace, Diderot's favorite Latin poet, along with Lucretius.[1] Horace's writings are the source of many an apt quotation in the *œuvre* from the *Encyclopédie* ("Tantum series junctaraque pollet, Tantum de medio sumptis accedit honoris")[2] to the *Supplément au voyage de Bougainville* ("At quanto meliora monet, pugnantiaque istis, Dives opis Naturae suae, tu si modo recte Dispensare velis, ac non fugienda petendis Immiscere! Tuo vitio rerumne labores, Nil referre putas?").[3] In *Rameau's Nephew* the quotation chosen is "Vertumnis, quotquot sunt, natus iniquis." The line may be roughly translated as: "Born under the baleful influence of Vertumnis," Vertumnis being the Roman god of chance.[4]

The allusion to Horace has two purposes. First, it inscribes Diderot's story in a literary tradition of value and prestige.[5] The tradition is, as Jean Marmier has observed in his indispensable *Horace au dix-septième siècle en France,* Roman satire.[6] Here is an exemplary form of comic writing, a model, in the eyes of cultured readers, of decorum and taste.[7] Epigraphs also have a second, more practical, side. They alert the reader—whose ability to decipher the Latin tag and place it in an appropriate frame of reference is an unstated assumption of the "rhetoric" of epigraphs—to the subject or topos used in the text.

The subject is the Saturnalia: the Roman feast day where, as Frazer said, "the distinction between the free and servile classes was abolished; slaves changed places with masters, convicts with judges, and the entire society of Rome was turned into a crazy-quilt or upside-down republic."[8] As indicated by the reference "HORAT., Lib. II, Satyr VII" appended to the quotation about Vertumnis, this passage is taken from the second book of Horace's *Satires* (satire seven). The text is generally referred to as the Saturnalian or "carnival" satire. It is the spirit of carnival, or a world turned upside down which—at first glance at least—provides the structure of Diderot's story.

Diderot uses two characters in his version of the Saturnalia. They are "Lui" and "Moi." The fact that Moi has no last name, has indeed been reduced to the anonymity of a stressed pronoun, does not prevent the reader from forming a clear opinion as to who such a person is. The confidence with which Moi introduces himself and his disdain for Lui mark him off as a gentleman-philosopher. Whatever the subject raised in his discussions with Lui—politics and love, taste and philosophy, as they are identified on the first page of the text—Moi upholds the conservatism of the class on whose behalf he speaks. He is a royalist in politics, a lover of the classics whose views on literature emphasize connections between art and morality, and, as well, a *père de famille,* much interested in educational plans for his daughter and her future prospects.

Moi's values place him solidly in the mold of the straight-man required by comedy. Though they earn him the respect of the amateur who might read Diderot's story (for whom views of this kind are expressions of common sense), their effect on Lui is quite different. To the latter, Moi's attitudes do not reflect intelligence or virtue. They are signs of blinkered conformity, shallow judgment, the mediocrity of one who has been reduced to the category of human beings Lui calls *espèces*.

Lui is not an *espèce*. He is the nephew of Jean-François Rameau, eighteenth-century France's greatest musical theorist and one of her finest opera composers.[9] Yet it is hard not to see him as an oddity in his own right. For he can be found, the narrator says, in tattered hand-me-downs and rags one day, and the next dressed like a minister about to call on the King. Lui consorts with street musicians, coachmen, and social marginals. His outlook on existence is a crude *Lebensphilosophie* at the opposite pole of Moi's epicureanism. One is in fact to regard him not so much as a curiosity, a common enough sight in Diderot's time as now, but, as Diderot's narrator specifically states, a freak:

> ...un des plus bizarres personnages de ce pais ou Dieu n'en a pas laissé manquer. C'est un composé de hauteur et de bassesse, de bon sens et de deraison. Il faut que les notions de l'honnete et du deshonnete soient bien etrangement brouillées dans sa tete; car il montre ce que la nature lui a donné de bonnes qualités, sans ostentation, et ce qu'il en a reçu de mauvaises, sans pudeur.[10]

The meeting between Lui and Moi dramatizes a play of impossible opposites typical of many comic writings of the French Enlightenment. It emphasizes the kind of *dialogue des sourds* to which such encounters usually lead: a French naval chaplain, for example, being unlikely to convince a Tahitian of the superiority of Paris over a tropical island—as we know from *Le Supplément au voyage de Bougainville*—or, in *Candide,* a Manichean able to win over a deist to a repetitive pattern of history rather than a logical one. Little time is lost in getting the movement of such an encounter under way.

The early pages of the dialogue, for example, have Lui asking Moi questions about genius, a key interest of classical aesthetics and literature. Yet Lui neglects to mention a central aspect of this subject. It is the truism, for the neoclassical mind, that genius is allied with ethics. What Lui concentrates on instead are links between genius and immorality.[11] Nor is the example he uses to make his point a typical one. It involves Racine, France's greatest literary figure, the reason for her standing as the successor to Greece and Rome and yet, as Lui puts it, "a bad father and a faithless friend."[12]

Lui's use of pantomime or dumb-acting is no less striking. The art seems inappropriate in a philosophical encounter of an Horatian kind. Even more puzzling are the subjects Lui acts out. They include music lovers nodding off to sleep as the curtain goes up on a new opera performance, a virtuoso pianist warming up at the keyboard, or opportunists speculating on how to apologize to various "goddesses" of society. These caricatures are rendered with an unusual kind of violence which makes Moi uneasy. They portend encroachments on his privacy. Soon, in fact, Moi speaks the first of what Roger Laufer has called a "confession of discomfiture":[13]

> Je l'ecoutois; et a mesure qu'il faisoit la scene du proxenete et de la jeune fille qu'il seduisoit; l'ame agitée de deux mouvements opposés, je

> ne scavois si je m'abandonnerois a l'envie de rire, ou au transport de l'indignation. Je soufrois. Vingt fois un éclat de rire empecha ma colere d'eclater; vingt fois la colere qui s'elevoit au fond de mon cœur se termina par un eclat de rire. J'etois confondu de tant de sagacité, et de tant de bassesse; d'idées si justes et alternativement si fausses; d'une perversité si generale de sentiments, d'une turpitude si complette, et d'une franchise si peu commune. Il s'apercut du conflict qui se passoit en moi: Qu'avez vous? me dit-il.[14]

Further assaults on Moi's dignity follow with little let-up. The next part of the chat between philosopher and bohemian moves from general problems of art or ethics to study of instances of genius and evil. One case involves the man known as the "Renegade of Avignon." He posed as the friend of a wealthy Jewish businessman, gained the latter's confidence, stole the contents of his house, and then, as a way of revealing a flair for cruelty worthy of a great artist, betrayed him to the Inquisition and a fate where, "quelques jours apres, on fit un beau feu de joye."[15]

Bouret is another connoisseur of evil, though on a less flamboyant scale. His talent lay in the use of masks. It allowed him, after various experiments of a Pavlovian kind, to turn a dog he loved against him and into the faithful pet of a new owner, the Keeper of the Seals, the whole experience serving to illustrate a tampering with natural law and a play of subjectivism and irony.[16]

These stories are odd indeed. They describe events which are morally dubious, yet not without aesthetic interest. Involved here is imaginative energy and the kind of isolation associated with the sensibility of artists. The uncanny feeling conveyed by such anecdotes soon gets to Moi, as his second "outburst" makes clear:

> Je ne scavois, moi, si je devois rester ou fuir, rire ou m'indigner. Je restai, dans le dessein de tourner la conversation sur quelque autre sujet qui chassat de mon ame l'horreur dont elle étoit remplie. Je commençois a supporter avec peine la presence d'un homme qui discutoit une action horrible, un execrable forfait, comme un connoisseur en peinture ou en poesie, examine les beautés d'un ouvrage de gout; ou comme un moraliste ou un historien releve et fait eclater les circonstances d'une action heroique. Je devins sombre, malgré moi. Il s'en aperçut et me dit:

> Lui.— Qu'avez vous? est ce que vous vous trouvez mal?
> Moi.— Un peu; mais cela passera.[17]

Moi's trial, though, is far from over. The next section of *Rameau's Nephew* brings up a subject even more damaging to his self-esteem. It is opera. What Lui warms to here is an account of the visit to Paris in the mid-1750s of a troupe of Italian opera singers whose "buffa" style of performing and singing divided operagoers of the time into two competing camps. The first supported French music, as represented by Lully and Rameau's uncle. The second, more radical wing, backed Italy and composers like Pergolesi and Duni. The conflict has come to be known as the *Querelle des bouffons* or "War of the Buffoni." It is a musical updating or variation on the theme of the Battle of the Books which ushered in the century.[18]

Lui's mastery of opera is much in evidence as he puts Moi through a kind of catechism of music. He stresses, for example, the feebleness of French as a musical language when compared to Italian. The one is nasal, cold, inseparable from a declamatory style which turns opera into a poor version of classical tragedy. Italian, by contrast, is naturally musical, revelling in dramatic markings throughout its "score" and not merely in isolated moments. It possesses what Lui calls the rights of "le vrai, le bon, le beau":

> A d'autres, a d'autres. On nous accoutumera a l'imitation des accents de la passion ou des phenomenes de la nature, par le chant et la voix, par l'instrument, car voila toute l'etendue de l'objet de la musique, et nous conserverons notre gout pour les vols, les lances, les gloires, les triomphes, les victoires? *Va t-en voir, s'ils viennent, Jean.* Ils ont imaginé qu'ils pleureroient ou riroient a des scenes de tragedie ou de comedie, musiquées; qu'on porteroit a leurs oreilles, les accents de la fureur, de la haine, de la jalousie, les vraies plaintes de l'amour, les ironies, les plaisanteries du théatre italien ou françois; et qu'ils resteroient admirateurs de *Ragonde* et de *Platée*. Je t'en reponds: tarare, ponpon; qu'ils eprouveroient sans cesse, avec quelle facilité, quelle flexibilité, quelle mollesse, l'harmonie, la prosodie, les ellipses, les inversions de la langue italienne se pretoient a l'art, au mouvement, a l'expression, aux tours du chant, et a la valeur mesurée des sons, et qu'ils continueroient d'ignorer combien la leur est roide, sourde, lourde, pesante, pedantesque et monotone. Eh oui, oui. Ils se sont persuadé

> qu'apres avoir melé leurs larmes aux pleurs d'une mere qui se desole sur la mort de son fils; apres avoir fremi de l'ordre d'un tyran qui ordonne un meurtre; ils ne s'ennuieroient pas de leur feerie, de leur insipide mithologie, de leurs petits madrigaux douceureux qui ne marquent pas moins le mauvais gout du poete, que la misere de l'art qui s'en accommode. Les bonnes gens! cela n'est pas et ne peut etre. Le vrai, le bon, le beau ont leurs droits. On les conteste, mais on finit par admirer.[19]

Lui asks Moi to think too about the difference between melody and harmony. Harmony—the essence of French musical tradition—is claimed by Lui to be at best a mathematical ordering of related tonalities. Melody, by contrast, the main characteristic of Italian opera, encourages lyricism and the fullness of sound Italian music seems best able to convey. He also discusses the importance of accent or stress, as conveyed in a maxim found in most eighteenth-century discussions of music from Rousseau's *Dictionnaire de musique* to Diderot's own numerous writings on musical themes, about accent being the seedbed of musical expression: *Musices seminarium accentus*.[20]

The lesson ends with a lively account of the differences between reading and speaking and how it is possible even for so parched a tongue as French to attain dramatic color when articulated in moments of great stress:

> Quiconque avoit ecouté un gueux lui demander l'aumone dans la rue, un homme dans le transport de la colere, une femme jalouse et furieuse, un amant desesperé, un flatteur, oui un flatteur radoucissant son ton, trainant ses sillabes, d'une voix mielleuse; en un mot une Passion, n'importe laquelle, pourvu que par son energie, elle meritât de servir de modele au musicien, auroit du s'apercevoir de deux choses: l'une que les sillabes, longues ou breves, n'ont aucune durée fixe, pas meme de rapport determiné entre leurs durees; que la passion dispose de la prosodie, presque comme il lui plait; qu'elle execute les plus grands intervalles, et que celui qui s'ecrie dans le fort de sa douleur: Ah, malheureux que je suis, monte la sillabe d'exclamation au ton le plus elevé et le plus aigu, et descend les autres aux tons les plus graves et les plus bas, faisant l'octave ou meme un plus grand intervalle, et donnant a chaque son la quantité qui convient au tour de la melodie; sans que l'oreille soit offensée, sans que ni la sillabe longue, ni la sillabe breve aient conservé la longueur ou la brieveté du discours tranquille.[21]

A musical illustration accompanies this introduction to Italian opera. It is the one that has come to be known as *l'homme orchestre* scene. Here Rameau becomes a *buffa* singer. He chants, dances, bounds forth as though taken with a musical fit, and gives his pupil an unexpected taste of the new style of opera he wants to introduce him to.

The passage is the high point of *Rameau's Nephew,* and is underscored as such by the fact that the chess players at the Café de la Régence (the place where Lui and Moi met to begin their chat) stop playing their game and form a circle around Lui as though they were part of an involuntary chorus. Its purpose is to reveal the unusual comic turnabout of Saturnalia. Moi, who is the apparent philosopher, has been demoted to the status of a fool or *stultus,* while Lui, the bohemian outlaw, is now crowned as a wise man or sage.

Moi fully deserves this change in rank. He has shown his clumsiness on all too many occasions. His views on art are those of a bygone era. A deafness to Italian opera denies him access to one of the century's great aesthetic forms. One is to view him at best as a comic figure to be dodged through Lui's superior balletic skills. An aspiring philosopher, or would-be sage: these are the titles which suit Moi best. Indeed at the end of the satire his confusion is such that he withdraws from serious conversation altogether. He repeats questions he had asked at the beginning of his conversation with Lui, espouses a mock Rousseauism thoroughly out of character with his earlier beliefs, and speaks of the pleasures of retreating, like Diogenes, into a barrel. Here he can survey with appropriate contempt (and bare feet) a world he can no longer understand or cope with. "Je veux mourir," he concludes, "si cela ne vaudroit mieux que de ramper, de s'avilir, et de se prostituer."[22]

Lui, by contrast, could not be in finer fettle. He has demolished Moi with little visible effort. The encounter has allowed him to perfect a pantomime routine or two and scrape together some needed dinner invitations as well. The closing pages of the text show him in full command of the situation. "I hear the bell announcing the new opera," he says. "I have no intention of missing it." Lui pirouettes, takes leave of his temporary partner and, in the last line of the book, delivers the *coup de grâce* to philosophical discussion: "Rira bien qui rira le dernier."[23] He who laughs last laughs best.

∞ ∞ ∞

"Rira bien qui rira le dernier" is surely one of the more memorable boutades in a century rich in comic send-offs: "Cela est bien dit, mais il faut cultiver notre jardin" (*Candide*); "Je m'en étais bien douté (*Micromégas*); and the different endings of *Jacques le fataliste* which show Diderot's determined fatalist both marrying Denise and being thrown in prison ("les fers aux pieds et aux mains étendu sur la paille au fond d'un cachot obscur, se rappelant tout ce qu'il avait retenu des principes de la philosophie de son capitaine").

The phrase pays tribute to a literary work which, though founded on the mayhem of Saturnalia, has been able to exorcise anarchy through the reasonableness of comedy. In comedy, events like the demotion of Moi and the crowning of Lui occur on a regular basis. They do so, however, on one condition. The condition is that such violations of authority be understood as temporary. When the props and illusions of Saturnalia have worked their effect, the twenty-four-hour period of freedom which is carnival will also come to an end. Normal structures of society will be restored, and on a more solid basis than before. A kind of venting has occurred, a release in a harmless and fictitious way of tensions which, if allowed real expression, would threaten the body politic.

The rules for reading Diderot, no less binding for not as yet having been fully spelled out, advise one what to make of this story which has proceded like the chess game referred to on so many occasions in *Rameau's Nephew*: allowing for a battle between two philosophies set against each other like the black and white squares of the chessboard, numerous moves and feints, and, at the end, the checkmating of Moi through which the victory of society is celebrated.

It is not as a permanent structure able to bind the story to reason or common sense but a false front to be challenged and hollowed out by various ironies found in Diderot's story and which center storytelling on a mood of "dispersion and displacement."[24]

The long paragraph which comes after the line about "Vertumnis, quotquot sunt, natus iniquis," provides a first example of the technique. It is set off from the rest of the work by the fact that it is in prose and not, as by far the larger part of the story will be, in dramatic dialogue:

> Qu'il fasse beau, qu'il fasse laid, c'est mon habitude d'aller sur les cinq heures du soir me promener au Palais Royal. C'est moi qu'on voit, toujours seul, rêvant sur le banc d'Argenson. Je m'entretiens avec moi meme de politique, d'amour, de gout ou de philosophie. J'abandonne mon esprit a tout son libertinage. Je le laisse maitre de suivre la premiere idée sage ou folle qui se presente, comme on voit dans l'allée de Foy nos jeunes dissolus marcher sur les pas d'une courtisane a l'air eventé, au visage riant, a l'œil vif, au nez retroussé, quitter celle cy pour une autre, les attaquant toutes et ne s'attachant a aucune. Mes pensées, ce sont mes catins. Si le tems est trop froid, ou trop pluvieux, je me refugie au caffé de la Regence; la je m'amuse a voir jouer aux echecs. Paris est l'endroit du monde, et le caffé de la Regence est l'endroit de Paris où l'on joue le mieux a ce jeu. C'est chez Rey que font assaut Legal le profond, Philidor le subtil, le solide Mayot; qu'on voit les coups les plus surprenants, et qu'on entend les plus mauvais propos; car si l'on peut etre homme d'esprit et grand joueur d'echecs, comme Legal; on peut etre aussi un grand joueur d'echecs, et un sot, comme Foubert et Mayot. Un apres diner, j'étois la, regardant beaucoup, parlant peu, et ecoutant le moins que je pouvois; lorsque je fus abordé par un des plus bizarres personnages de ce pais ou Dieu n'en a pas laissé manquer. C'est un composé de hauteur et de bassesse, de bon sens et de deraison. Il faut que les notions de l'honnete et du deshonnete soient bien etrangement brouillées dans sa tete; car il montre ce que la nature lui a donné de bonnes qualités, sans ostentation, et ce qu'il en a reçu de mauvaises, sans pudeur.[25]

The outer shell of the passage is conventional enough. Sentences are structured in a present tense meant to suggest a way of seeing things *sub specie aeternitatis*. "Paris est l'endroit du monde, et le caffé de la Regence est l'endroit de Paris où l'on joue le mieux a ce jeu." "C'est un composé de hauteur et de bassesse, de bon sens et de deraison."[26] Antitheses like *beau* and *laid, honnete* and *deshonnete* abound. They convey the binary opposites which are central to classical discourse.[27] And, of course, the dominant metaphor is chess. Chess is an aristocratic game with knights, pawns, kings, and queens drawn up in battle array, stretched out on a board according to their position, colored squares symbolizing limits and constraint, and, arching over the game, those "great strokes of audacity and genius," which emphasize the generosity of imaginative play.

Yet hidden in this passage still heavy with the scent of the past, are features of a more disruptive and modern kind. Syntax is one of them. Though the passage is conceived as a *période,* or account of a subject whose complexity is such as to require a full-scale description of its features, it lacks the temporal development or connecting links generally expected in such passages.[28]

Weak coordinates like semicolons take precedence over words like *car, ainsi que,* or *puisque.* Loose verb forms like present participles (*regardant beaucoup, parlant peu*) are much in evidence, creating effects of a disjunctive and parataxical kind.[29] Vocabulary is similarly odd. Though many words refer to abstractions like *goût* or *philosophie,* others bring into play references of a more problematical nature. *Composé* is one such word. The term is scientific and out of place in a *galant* context.[30] The passage contains a large number of clichés ("C'est chez Rey que font assaut Legal le profond, Philidor le subtil, le solide Mayot...") meant to give the text a burlesque tone and to challenge tradition or past achievement.[31] The passage even lacks a clear sense of time. The main reference of the text is to an *après-dîner.*[32] The word evokes *an* afternoon rather than a specific afternoon (a moment somewhere between noon and five). Taken as a whole, the mood created by the passage is not clarity at all but indeterminacy and flux: a moment which flits back and forth between different periods of time without achieving any distinct order.

Other parts of the work pick up the flavor of this statement as though it were a curtain raiser or overture. Characterization is one of them. If Moi provides an example of the psychology of humors and a view of self which harks back to Theophrastus or—a key French influence—La Bruyère, the same cannot be said of Lui.[33] The latter enjoys a protean status seemingly outside the grid of *caractères.* His life is subject to unaccountable shifts between outcast and musical virtuoso, street performer, and *homme orchestre.* These changes reflect the reality of a musician's life in eighteenth-century France, to be sure. They also point to something else. It is a conception of being as problematical and open, the more interesting and poignant because it escapes categorization and, in the final analysis, understanding.

Subject matter is similarly unusual. It breaks away from the mood of *persiflage* established in early aphorisms like "Mes pensées ce sont mes catins"[34] to concentrate instead on more serious concerns raised by opera and music. Among them are issues touching on the nature of language and the origin of literary representation. Music is also the source of a good deal of speculation on *les anciens et les modernes.*

Narrative structure shows an even more emphatic way of distancing satire from Horace. It reveals the hold of a form of storytelling foreign to Roman satire. The mode is first-person narration in a manner usually associated with the novel.

Moi is, of course, at the heart of this narration. His early comments about how he would go for a stroll rain or shine in the Palais Royal, hold discussions with himself on politics, love, taste, or philosophy, and let his thoughts wander in complete abandon, display an almost textbook rendering of first-person pronouns. Virtually all of the grammatical possibilities of this form (whose validation of the private and the subjective stands in opposition to the more impersonal "il") make an appearance in the French version of the text. "Je" is one example, as seen in the sentence, "J'abandonne mon esprit a tout son libertinage." Possessives are numerous: "mon esprit," "mes pensées," "mon habitude." Stressed or intense pronouns like "C'est moi" broaden the list. It is completed by a full play of reflexives throughout the passage, but with greatest concentration at the beginning: "Je m'entretiens avec moi meme de politique, d'amour, de gout ou de philosophie."[35]

The purpose of this flood of pronouns is the one which governs all forms of a repetitive kind. It is intensification.[36] By means of these references the narrator draws attention to his unique status. He is the fellow who has come down from his lodgings, been engaged by Lui in conversation, and been put through the kind of comic sacrifice necessary for the telling of *Rameau's Nephew* and the equilibrium to which it has led. Having endured Lui's onslaughts on his dignity and character, been reduced to the condition of an *espèce,* the narrator can, once Saturnalia has ended, turn the tables on Lui. He will write up his encounter with Rameau in a literary text. Here he will decide which of the latter's sallies to include and which ones to leave out, which tone to give their chat: how to present it, in short, to his readers.

This self-assurance is not, however, without its own problematical side. For the narrator's voice is not the only one in *Rameau's Nephew*. Once he has introduced the main protagonists of the story and set out its organizing metaphors and themes, the narrator disappears. He returns only when vague stage directions are called for, or comments on how a given scene is to be interpreted (information usually set off from the rest of the text by brackets, as with remarks like: "Puis il se remettoit a chanter l'ouverture des *Indes galantes,* et l'air *Profonds abymes;* et il ajoutoit...").[37]

By far the greater part of the story is told through a second voice. This voice is "Lui and Moi." Lui is the term used throughout the text to refer to "Rameau's nephew." Moi is a new designation. The narrator uses it as a *dédoublement* through which he can shed his standing as an observer or judge and enter more directly into the spirit of Saturnalia, emphasizing in the process the reliability of what took place and his own honesty.[38]

Lui and Moi speak in dialogue. Statements are set down without quotation marks or attribution. They are printed with the directness of an acting script and made part of an order of time which is not the old-fashioned one of the past definite but the more modern one of the spoken present. As Peter France has observed, dialogue is an "order of discourse" in Diderot's fictions.[39] It animates all of the great stories from the *Supplément au voyage de Bougainville, L'Entretien sur le fils naturel* to longer narratives like *Jacques le fataliste* (a novel in dialogue form) and *Le Rêve de d'Alembert*—the latter a work which is roughly the same length as *Le Neveu de Rameau* and closely allied to many of its interests.

The advantages of dialogue are many. Dialogue describes events which are still in the process of taking shape, as yet unmastered by the retrospective or mature mode which is the special province of the novel. Intimacy is another feature. Dialogue stresses idiosyncracies of speech, personal rhythms of delivery, and (in *Rameau's Nephew* at least) details of a distinctly autobiographical kind: days spent in cafés with Rousseau, scenes about the proper way of educating daughters where one cannot but discern the shadow of Madame de Vandeul, and, in the early pages, allusions to the creased waistcoats and darned stockings "Diderot" would wear when he went out in Paris to give lessons in music or mathematics. Dialogue is also innately theatrical. Interruptions and pauses are frequent. Moments of silence and reversals draw out its range. They give it color and the unpredictability of spoken language.

Two kinds of narrative reporting thus make up the body of *Rameau's Nephew*. The first is the discourse of the narrator. The other is that of Lui and Moi. The narrator speaks with authority and purpose. His voice emphasizes tradition, common sense, the weight of an event that has been understood and made part of a single focus of reporting. The formalists call this kind of discourse "monologic."[40]

The speech of Lui and Moi lacks this solidity. It suggests discussions of a "dialogic" kind (the latter term serving as a counterpart to monologic).[41] Dialogue tends to describe events outside the dictionary of beliefs of a given society. It underscores a spoken voice which cannot be pinned down to a single authoritative source or "dépôt de vérité." One is to view dialogic conversation as plural or ironic.

What is striking about these modes of reporting is not only their differences—the one historical and objective, the other subjective and personal—but their incompatibility. No way exists to bring such competing forms into a single order or meaning. For all modes which might have done so—Horatian satire, the Saturnalia, or the chessboard—have already been challenged and, to no small extent, clouded over through the ironies of Diderot's story.

Monologic and dialogic speech thus confront each other across an empty space uncannily reminiscent of the dead-end conversations between Mr. Philosopher and Rameau. The effect of this blankness is far more serious than a momentary disagreement about art or education. It calls into question the arrangement of the story of *Le Neveu de Rameau* as a whole, suggesting in fact the inability of the narrator to grant the tale an overall unity or coherence of design.[42]

∞ ∞ ∞

What has occurred in *Rameau's Nephew*, then, summarizing the story of Lui and Moi as it has evolved to this point, is a displacement of the

Horatian example on which Diderot's story began and which provided it (to outer appearances at least) with its comic momentum, narrative order, and sense of tradition.

Ironies concealed in the work decenter this arrangement. They introduce interests of a far more problematical and unstable kind. Discourse in the style of "fillies and follies" shifts to discussions dominated by music and the new interests of opera. The fluent voice of "M. le philosophe" speaking on behalf of a community of gentlemen scholars is changed into the masked narration of Lui and Moi. Even the dualities of the Saturnalia undergo change. They fall away from the sharp outlines and contrasts of master and slave (everyday life and *Fête*) to embrace a more indeterminate region best described by the phrase "classical plural."

At issue here, Barthes says, is a text which lacks an origin or distinct point of view, a writing whose indeterminacies are in some way symbolic of the modern:

> ...in the classic text the majority of the utterances are assigned an origin, we can identify their parentage, who is speaking: either a consciousness (of a character, of the author) or a culture (the anonymous is still an origin, a voice: the voice we find, for example, in the gnomic code); however, it may happen that in the classic text, always haunted by the appropriation of speech, the voice gets lost, as though it had leaked out through a hole in the discourse. The best way to conceive the classical plural is then to listen to the text as an iridescent exchange carried on by multiple voices, on different wavelengths and subject from time to time to a sudden *dissolve,* leaving a gap which enables the utterance to shift from one point of view to another, without warning: the writing is set up across this tonal instability (which in the modern text becomes atonality), which makes it a glistening texture of ephemeral origins.[43]

The Socratic interests which guide Diderot's *œuvre* will not, of course, stop at this blurred state but will exact more demanding and critically purposeful strategies of irony. One section of Diderot's story always enjoys special standing in this regard. It is the story within a story or *emboîtement*. These are staples of self-conscious writing from *Tristram Shandy* to *Don Quixote* (and many a text in Diderot as well).

Such tales are not mere anecdotes. Stories within a story demonstrate the freedom of narrative, its openness to blank pages, doodles, runaway horses, and what Sterne was to call "curtains falling over the scene." They also enjoy a distinctly Socratic status. For *emboîtements* are hidden pockets of truth. They provide examples of counter-verities buried, according to Socratic lore, in what is, to outer appearances, a slight neoclassical *facétie*.

Le Neveu de Rameau contains many references to these Socratic procedures (as well as several stories within a story). *Grain de levain* is one such reference. The term suggests a leavening agent possessed of unique critical force. *Molécule* is another. The allusion points up the vitalistic materialism central to Diderot's view of nature. The most potent term, though, is *le dieu étranger* or foreign idol. Here is a clear articulation of Socratic subversion:

> L'empire de la nature, et de ma trinité, contre laquelle les portes de l'enfer ne prevaudront jamais: le vrai qui est le pere, et qui engendre le bon qui est le fils; d'ou procede le beau qui est le saint esprit, s'établit tout doucement. Le dieu etranger se place humblement a coté de l'idole du pais; peu a peu, il s'y affermit; un beau jour il pousse du coude son camarade; et patatras, voila l'idole en bas. C'est comme cela qu'on dit que les Jesuites ont planté le christianisme a la Chine et aux Indes. Et ces Jansenistes ont beau dire, cette methode politique qui marche a son but, sans bruit, sans effusion de sang, sans martyr sans un toupet de cheveux arraché, me semble la meilleure.[44]

One story within a story is central to Diderot's text. It can be found in the middle section of *Le Neveu de Rameau* and has engaged the attention of all critics who have written on Diderot, from nineteenth-century readers like Lord Morley or Rosenkranz to the many scholars listed in Spears's invaluable *Bibliographie de Diderot*. The scene is the one that has come to be known as *l'homme orchestre*.

The passage shows a chaos of forms from pantomime to philosophical dialogue. Its tone is mixed and erratic; the comic streak contains a blend of Voltairian farce and cruel self-mimicry. Even the term *"homme orchestre"* is problematical. "One-man band" is surely too flippant. "Orchestra man" is clumsy (and indebted to a musical form whose eighteenth-century version is hardly comparable to the orchestra of today). Even if, as is desirable, "one-man show" is used to translate *l'homme orchestre,* the phrase only barely conveys the novelty and shock of Rameau's art.

Yet there can be little question as to the importance of this scene or the role it plays in Diderot's story. With the appearance of Lui in the one-man show a proper degree of critical temperature has been found to convey the Socratic ironies which sustain Diderot's text. Satire will now leave the blurred framework of the "classical plural" that gave Diderot's work so comfortable and reassuring a feeling. Ironic contrasts will now involve more violent juxtapositions between new and old, triviality and invention. They will, in fact, dramatize a full-scale war.

On the one hand stands the beleaguered world of Horace and the chessboard on which Lui and Moi performed various moves and ploys. On the other are the newer interests introduced by Lui. Pantomime is one such interest, to be sure. So too is dialogue and the kind of immoralism described by Herbert Josephs as defining a person who has "learned to distinguish between what a man seems to feel and what he does feel;" a person "adept at imitating all the external signs of human behavior, at masking himself beneath the language, the intonations, and the gestures of whatever vice or virtue the needs of his parasitic existence may call upon him to display."[45] Over the *homme orchestre* scene looms a motif even more critical to its meaning. The motif is Italian opera and musical drama. It is to an analysis of this passage, and its place in the story of *Le Neveu de Rameau,* that we now turn.

III

L'homme orchestre

THE SCENE OF *L'HOMME ORCHESTRE* comes suddenly over *Le Neveu de Rameau*. It floods a mild-mannered philosophical chat between Lui and Moi with an example of mime, or dumb-acting, designed as an improvisation on Italian opera:

> Et puis le voila qui se met a se promener, en murmurant dans son gosier, quelquesuns des airs de *l'Isle des Fous,* du *Peintre amoureux de son modele,* du *Maréchal ferrant,* de *la Plaideuse,* et de tems en tems, il s'ecrioit, en levant les mains et les yeux au ciel; si cela est beau, mordieu! Si cela est beau! Comment peut-on porter a sa tete une paire d'oreilles et faire une pareille question. Il commencoit a entrer en passion, et a chanter tout bas. Il elevoit le ton, a mesure qu'il se passionnoit davantage; vinrent ensuite, les gestes, les grimaces du visage et les contorsions du corps; et je dis, bon; voila la tete qui se perd, et quelque scène nouvelle qui se prepare; en effet il part d'un eclat de voix, *Je suis un pauvre miserable...Monseigneur, monseigneur, laissez moi partir...O terre, reçois mon or; conserve bien mon tresor...Mon ame, mon ame, ma vie! O terre!...La voila le petit ami; le voila le petit ami!* - *Aspettare e non venire...A Zerbina penserete... Sempre in contrasti con te si sta...* Il entassoit et brouilloit ensemble trente airs, italiens, françois, tragiques, comiques, de toutes sortes de caracteres; tantot avec une voix de basse-taille, il descendoit jusqu'aux enfers; tantot s'egosillant, et contrefaisant le fausset, il dechiroit le haut des airs, imitant de la demarche, du maintien, du geste, les differents personnages chantants; successivement furieux, radouci, imperieux, ricaneur. Ici, c'est une jeune fille qui pleure et il en rend toute la minauderie; la il est pretre, il est roi, il est tyran, il menace, il commande, il s'emporte; il est esclave, il obéit. Il s'apaise, il se

desole, il se plaint, il rit; jamais hors de ton, de mesure, du sens des paroles et du caractere de l'air. Tous les pousse-bois avoient quitté leurs echiquiers et s'etoient rassemblés autour de lui. Les fenetres du caffé etoient occupées, en dehors, par les passants qui s'etoient arretés au bruit. On faisoit des eclats de rire a entrouvrir le plafond. Lui n'apercevoit rien; il continuoit, saisi d'une alienation d'esprit, d'un enthousiasme si voisin de la folie, qu'il est incertain qu'il en revienne; s'il ne faudra pas le jetter dans un fiacre, et le mener droit aux Petites Maisons.[1]

Mime is, to be sure, a major interest of Diderot's story. It reveals the hold of many aesthetic influences from the *Commedia dell'arte* (an ever-present *philosophe* interest), intermezzi taken from French comic opera, and the *théâtre de la foire*.[2] The presence of these forms turns Diderot's work into the most "pantomimic" of narratives in French literature, as well as a textbook of pre-revolutionary comic techniques.

By far the majority of the mime episodes found in the story are mimetic or realistic in intent. Whatever the subject involved—Rameau drinking wine, clicking his tongue in anticipation of the pleasure of swallowing some rare vintage, imitating his wife's walk, "head held high, playing with a fan, wriggling his behind in a most amusing and ridiculous caricature of our little tarts," a take-off on a miser hugging golden ducats—gesture indeed does the talking.[3] Through bodily movement, a mannerism which sums up a target is isolated and given the exaggeration which ensures that the viewer will recognize the subject of the parody and take part in the laughter such caricature is meant to encourage.[4]

Realistic portraits of this kind can be found in *l'homme orchestre* scene too. They include the picture of a young girl simpering; a priest threatening, commanding, flying into a rage; and that part of the passage which shows Rameau playing all the instruments of a musical orchestra: "With cheeks puffed out and a hoarse, dark tone, he did the horns and the bassoons, a bright nasal tone for the oboes, quickening his voice with incredible agility for the stringed instruments to which he tried to get the closest approximations, using whistling to imitate the sound of a recorder and a kind of cooing to do the flutes."[5]

Yet the originality of the passage, the reason for its standing as a central text in the history of eighteenth-century aesthetics, derives from

Diderot's use of mime in another context. It is as a means of describing subjects which transcend the mimetic. "Night with its shadows" is one such subject, projecting as it does on the stage of the Café de la Régence a subject which cannot be looked up in eighteenth-century guides to pantomime routines. "Birds falling silent at eventide" is another. It asks the actor to give form to a non-representative, even invisible, theme. In "shrieks of the dying mingling with the howling of sunset" can be found another instance of a subject outside traditional acting routines. Even more unusual is pantomime called upon to describe silence: "...car le silence meme se peint par des sons."[6]

Subjects like these are certainly out of place in an art form traditionally thought of as related to minor comic entertainments or lazzi routines. Nor is their presence an accident. Through them, Diderot is able to give life to a favored way of introducing novel concepts of aesthetics. It is as puzzles or conundrums.

La Lettre sur les sourds et muets, "without doubt one of the most farsighted and egregiously original texts to come from his pen," provides an exemplary instance of the technique.[7] Here Diderot speaks of a musical instrument known as a *piano à rubans*. This piano had ribbons on the keyboard instead of keys. Each ribbon was tuned to the color of a given musical tonality. When a piece was played, the instrument provided a kind of operatic effect. It allowed for a composition to be heard and seen at the same time, and to create a feeling of stunned amazement in the listener:

> Ah! Monsieur, vous ne devinerez jamais l'impression que cette machine fit sur lui et moins encore les pensées qui lui vinrent...Il crut tout d'un coup qu'il avoit saisi ce que c'étoit que la musique et tous les instruments de musique. Il crut que la musique étoit une façon particulière de communiquer la pensée.[8]

In astonishment lies of course a desired reaction. When faced with hybrids like the *piano à rubans* (or other exceptions to hierarchies and rules), viewers cannot withdraw into the indifference described by Rousseau in *La Lettre à d'Alembert sur les spectacles* as allowing them, after having purchased a ticket for a theatrical performance, to recline in their seats for an hour or two, enjoy the beauty of a work of art and return home as though nothing had happened.⁹ Examples like the *piano à rubans* impose their novelty with the force of truth. They create a condition not unlike that experienced by Moi. It is the state of an involuntary participant in an aesthetic event which violates traditional norms, and yet whose fascination is such that it can only be avoided (to cite a somewhat folksy example given by Diderot) if the listener stuffs his fingers in his ears, or, a prescription taken from *La Lettre à d'Alembert,* a blindfold is placed over his eyes.¹⁰

Similar educational interests sustain the *homme orchestre* scene. The subject raised here, however, is more demanding than synaesthesia. At issue is a meditation on aesthetic performance or *spectacle:* the theme which has been hovering over *Rameau's Nephew* in three critical references. They are Italian opera; the Saturnalia (a kind of public theater where society reenacts its founding and, some might say, arbitrary status); and chess. The latter is also a public event. Chess is played at the Café de la Régence, a haunt of woodpushers and idlers. It requires players or partners. The chessboard provides a mimetic representation of all ranks and classes of society from pawn to king.

Spectacle has many meanings in English which make it hard to pin down. Yet the sense in which the word is used in *Rameau's Nephew* is not in the least ambiguous. It is the one defined in two major contributions to the subject: Rousseau's *Lettre à d'Alembert sur les spectacles* and d'Alembert's *Encyclopédie* article "Genève." *Spectacle* means a meditation on theater and culture in the widest sense. An inquiry into the origins of theater is an integral part of the concern, to be sure. Reflection on the role of audience and actors is another. The deeper point of such theorizing is to open up a vista on nature. Nature is for the eighteenth-century mind the source of aesthetic value and meaning.¹¹

∞ ∞ ∞

The view of *spectacle* espoused in *Le Neveu de Rameau* closely follows theories articulated by Diderot in *Encyclopédie* articles like "Scythes," "Ethiopiens," and "Génie" and the *Discours sur la poésie dramatique* (texts roughly contemporary with the writing of the story of Lui and Moi). It is theater as primitive experience, allied with a search for the romantic sublime.[12]

The subject of dramatic poetry, Diderot was to claim in these writings, is the disaffiliated and the wild. Poetic subjects evoke ruins, waterfalls cascading down mountains, storm-tossed waves, the horror of night. In such topics can be found the energy of nature as yet unenfeebled by civilization. In them too lies the sublimity of an early state of imagination. As Diderot was to formulate the ideal in an often quoted and deservedly famous phrase, the realm of poetry is the anarchic and the barbarous: "La poésie veut quelque chose d'énorme et de barbare."[13]

Lui is, of course, at the center of this enthusiasm. He bounds forth on stage, puts himself through the contortions of mime, shouts, does imitations of French and Italian arias and, the narrator says, becomes a wild man or *énergumène:*

> ...criant, chantant, se demenant comme un forcené; faisant lui seul, les danseurs, les danseuses, les chanteurs, les chanteuses, tout un orchestre, tout un theatre lyrique, et se divisant en vingt roles divers, courant, s'arretant, avec l'air d'un energumene, etincellant des yeux, ecumant de la bouche.[14]

Energumène is a satiric term. It conveys the excitability and frenzy of a tub-thumper or ranter. Yet the word also has a more exacting meaning. It signifies demonic possession or frenzy. "Energumène," Fabre wrote in his notes to the edition of *Le Neveu de Rameau* (quoting from an article in the *Dictionnaire de Trévoux*), "possessed by the devil, requiring a kind of exorcism."[15]

Lui has but to appear on the "stage" of the Café de la Régence, to begin the first of his antics, for the kind of miraculous instant of theater spoken about by Diderot in *Jacques le fataliste* to occur. Here he says that if a real execution were to be held near a theater where a stage hanging was being put on, the theater would empty out on the spot. So too in *Rameau's Nephew.* Those engaged in playing chess at the Café de la Régence leave their game. Passers-by halt on the street. They press their faces against the window of the café and become spectators to Lui's art. The very city of

Paris, the center of French society, and, for Frenchmen, the world, comes to a dead stop.[16]

Lui's performance seems to justify this awe. The images his art portrays—temples being raised from the dust, whistling birds, the sounds of silence—are archaic. Their cross-breedings of genre reject the rules of classicism. His acting style is equally queer. It draws on an elementary physicality foreign to *bienséances* and uses the body less as a dead weight requiring sublimation through spoken language or the beauty of props than as a living stage.

As such, his art possesses the shock value of all modes which turn tradition and rules on their head. The sparseness of mime, for example—an aesthetic form peeled back to a single performer acting without script or prompter—indicts the extravagance of classical theater. The latter is an art of *dépouillement* or sobriety in name only. In reality it is overripe: dependent on chariots descending from the heavens, ornate constumes, and, outside the hall where an opera or a tragedy is being performed, carriages and servants which remind one that classical tragedy (or grand opera) is a mode of politics as well as aesthetics, indebted to a social order it provides spiritual legitimacy for and without whose patronage it would cease to exist.[17]

Mime takes on, too, the *comédien* or actor, a traditional butt of drama criticism. This expert in "lying and selling his soul" as Rousseau was to write in a celebrated passage of *La Lettre à d'Alembert*,[18] is sent packing with the first pirouettes of Lui much as his fellows at the French opera fled from the stage with the arrival of the *buffoni*. An actor's monotonous delivery of his lines, barely audible above the chattering in the loges, cannot keep pace with the "foaming" style of Lui. His gestures are wooden, lacking the movement of mime. And of course the dedication of a French *comédien* to the printed page and traditions of how verse is to be read deprives him of the energy of Lui's superior talent: an art held in check only by the limits of spontaneity.

Mime makes other points as well. The universality of dumb-acting challenges national prejudices which require that "pirate shows be put on in Tunis, vendettas in Sicily and in Goa the honor of burning heretics."[19] It restores aesthetic judgment to peasants, children, even the deaf and the dumb, in whose taste reposes a more natural way of responding to aesthetic expression (as well as, of course, an ideal theatrical audience). Mime subverts the unspoken contract between actor and audience which ensures that a faithful representation of the beliefs and values of a given time will be rewarded with a salary and, a key term in Rousseau, applause.[20] It calls into question the understanding that a performance given on a Monday will be repeated the following day or week in a manner closely approximating its first appearance. For mime is an unstable and fugitive form. It is played only once.

The more significant critical point of mime, of course, bears on language and the special place of French as an artistic medium. For mime is deaf to French. It is one of the ironies of Diderot that he records this indictment of French by means of an unexpected *dédoublement*. Only through a reading of the way in which Lui's antics are portrayed in the literary text called *Le Neveu de Rameau* can their full power be appreciated.

∞ ∞ ∞

Mais vous vous seriez echappé en eclats de rire, a la maniere dont il contrefaisoit les differents instruments. Avec des joues renflées et boufies, et un son rauque et sombre, il rendoit les cors et les bassons; il prenoit un son eclatant et nazillard pour les hautbois; precipitant sa voix avec une rapidité incroyable, pour les instruments a cordes dont il cherchoit les sons les plus approchés; il siffloit les petites flutes; il recouloit les traversieres, criant, chantant, se demenant comme un forcené; faisant lui seul, les danseurs, les danseuses, les chanteurs, les chanteuses, tout un orchestre, tout un theatre lyrique, et se divisant en vingt roles divers, courant, s'arretant, avec l'air d'un energumene, etincelant des yeux, ecumant de la bouche. Il faisoit une chaleur a perir; et la sueur qui suivoit les plis de son front et la longueur de ses joues, se meloit a la poudre de ses cheveux, ruisseloit et sillonnoit le haut de son habit. Que ne lui vis je pas faire? Il pleuroit, il rioit, il soupiroit; il regardoit, ou attendri, ou tranquille, ou furieux; c'etoit une femme qui se pame de douleur; c'etoit un malheureux livré a tout son desespoir; un temple qui s'eleve; des oiseaux qui se taisent au soleil couchant; des eaux qui murment [*sic*] dans un lieu solitaire et frais, ou qui descendent en torrents du haut des montagnes; un orage, une tempete, la plainte de ceux qui vont perir, melée au sifflement des vents, au fracas du tonnerre;

c'etoit la nuit, avec ses tenebres; c'etoit l'ombre et le silence; car le silence meme se peint par des sons. Sa tete etoit tout a fait perdue. Epuisé de fatigue, tel qu'un homme qui sort d'un profond sommeil ou d'une longue distraction; il resta immobile, stupide, etonné. Il tournoit ses regards autour de lui, comme un homme egaré qui cherche a reconnoitre le lieu ou il se trouve. Il attendoit le retour de ses forces et de ses esprits; il essuyoit machinalement son visage. Semblable a celui qui verroit a son reveil, son lit environné d'un grand nombre de personnes; dans un entier oubli ou dans une profonde ignorance de ce qu'il a fait, il s'ecria dans le premier moment: He bien, messieurs, qu'est ce qu'il y a? d'où viennent vos ris, et votre surprise? qu'est ce qu'il y a? Ensuite il ajouta, voila ce qu'on doit appeler de la musique et un musicien. Cependant, messieurs, il ne faut pas mepriser certains morceaux de Lulli. Qu'on fasse mieux la scene, *Ah! j'attendrai* sans changer les paroles; j'en defie. Il ne faut pas mepriser quelques endroits de Campra, les airs de violon de mon oncle, ses gavotes; ses entrées de soldats, de pretres, de sacrificateurs...*Pales flambeaux, nuit plus affreuse que les tenebres...Dieux du Tartare, Dieu de l'Oubli.* La, il enfloit sa voix; il soutenoit ses sons; les voisins se mettoient aux fenetres; nous mettions nos doigts dans nos oreilles. Il ajoutoit, c'est ici qu'il faut des poumons; un grand organe, un volume d'air. Mais avant peu, serviteur a l'Assomption; le careme et les Rois sont passés. Ils ne scavent pas encore ce qu'il faut mettre en musique, ni par consequent ce qui convient au musicien. La poesie lyrique est encore a naitre. Mais ils y viendront; a force d'entendre le Pergolese, le Saxon, Terradoglias, Trasetta, et les autres; a force de lire le Metastase, il faudra bien qu'ils y viennent.[21]

The passage quoted above could not strike Diderot's contemporaries (were they able to read it)[22] as a transcription from an alien tongue. Subject matter contributes to this strangeness to no small degree. It elevates Diderot's interest in change and flux—lovers professing eternal devotion beside trees already beginning to lose their bark and fall into decay—to an evocation of dissolution and change uncannily reminiscent of the more radical passages of *Le Rêve de d'Alembert*.[23] The mix of dialogue and silence is equally disconcerting. Even more revealing is the syntax of the text. Though ostensibly conceived in a style of Voltairian comedy, the passage rejects the rules of *philosophe* writing and the literary world which it endorses.

Philosophe satire is a violent genre indeed. Earthquakes, burnings at the stake, hosts thrown off bridges as a reward for their hospitality, shipwrecks and other disasters: here are standard topoi for works like *Candide* and *Zadig*. They illustrate the chaos of history and philosophical systems, to be sure. But such subjects have another purpose. They point up the serenity of *philosophe* irony: a mode in some way outside calamity, in fact, a symbol of reasonableness and order.

Over and above the pages of a work which invites the reader to reflect on the absurdity of Biscayens or Westphalians being whipped because they "ate lard" or chateaux thought to be magnificent because they contained "a few broken-down doors and a window here and there"[24] stands common sense. The latter challenges the absurdity of fiction. It reestablishes the certainty that French merchant ships cannot be held in the hands of giants, or Cunégonde allowed to be bayonneted, raped, sold into slavery, and a few chapters later, brought back in good health to discuss marriage plans with Candide.

Literary syntax provides an equally firm basis for order. However violent their subject matter, stories like *Candide* inevitably come back to clear sentences, balanced paragraphs and proper use of the *passé simple*. A smooth flow of chapters (though repetitive in content) ensures a solid literary structure. So too does the role of the narrator. The latter is a patrician voice above the fray of battle and the confusion of the *naïfs* on whose travels he reports. His comments emphasize an essential skepticism and irony. Man's intelligence is a small thing. He cannot master the problem of evil or come to any real understanding why it is that Manicheans drown in shipwrecks rather than believers in free will (or both at once). Such dilemmas lie beyond philosophy. Nor is recognition of this state a painful one. In it lie maturity and philosophical wisdom: the message, in many respects, of Candide's initiation into the world.[25]

This reasonableness of irony is absent in *Rameau's Nephew*. Nor is this due only to the presence of music or other interests which give Diderot's story an impressionistic side foreign to Voltaire. The drawing away from *philosophe* irony has to do rather with Diderot's use of comic irony. In his hands, irony is no longer an instrument of moral clarity and truth. It is a subversive tool directed at classical discourse and meaning.

32   SOCRATIC SATIRE

The device of parataxis present in the overture passage (as noted in an earlier chapter) is carried to an extreme degree of dislocation, even frenzy. Virtually all of the sentences in the passage quoted above are constructed in this manner and not, as was the case in the overture passage, a handful of them:

> Mais vous seriez echappé en eclats de rire, a la maniere dont il contrefaisoit les differents instruments. Avec des joues renflées et boufies, et un son rauque et sombre, il rendoit les cors et les bassons; il prenoit un son eclatant et nazillard pour les hautbois; precipitant sa voix avec une rapidité incroyable, pour les instruments a cordes dont il cherchoit les sons les plus approchés; il siffloit les petites flutes; il recouloit les traversières, criant, chantant, se demenant comme un forcené; faisant lui seul, les danseurs, les danseuses, les chanteurs, les chanteuses, tout un orchestre, tout un theatre lyrique, et se divisant en vingt roles divers, courant, s'arretant, avec l'air d'un energumene, etincelant des yeux, ecumant de la bouche.[26]

An excessive use of personal pronouns is to be noted as well. Their purpose is to remove Diderot's text from a playful musing on instability and flux[27] and bring it into a seemingly endless cycle of ironic self-creation and duplication:

> Ici, c'est une jeune fille qui pleure et il en rend toute la minauderie; la il est pretre, il est roi, il est tyran, il menace, il commande, il s'emporte, il est esclave, il obeit. Il s'apaise, il se desole, il se plaint, il rit; jamais hors de ton, de mesure, du sens des paroles et du caractere de l'air.[28]

Verb tenses add to the climate of stress. They reveal a preference for open or lax tenses like the present participle ("se divisant en vingt roles divers, courant, s'arretant, avec l'air d'un energumene, etincelant des yeux, ecumant de la bouche") and deny the stable focus of the *passé simple* or other historical tenses.

No less disturbing is what the author calls "musical writing." *Musiquer* is the verb he uses to describe this interest. The word is, as Fabre has pointed out, a neologism, unrecorded in contemporary editions of the French Academy. Diderot's narator uses it three times, though, and with clear dramatic emphasis: "Il n'y a pas six vers de suite...qu'on puisse musiquer;" "J'aimerais autant avoir à musiquer les maximes de La Rochefoucauld;" "Je musiquais, comme il plaît à Dieu."[29]

Musical writing dramatizes ironic contrasts between French and Italian, a language already suspect in the eyes of traditional readers because of its associations with the *buffoni*. It emphasizes intertextualities which are not only literary (a series of quotations from Horace, for example) but musical—"Je suis un misérable...Monseigneur, monseigneur, laissez-moi partir...O terre, reçois mon or; conserve bien mon trésor...Mon âme, mon âme, ma vie! O terre..."—thus giving the work a kind of operatic character foreign to satire. Above all, musical writing endows the passage of *l'homme orchestre* with the properties of Italian music: a model which is not a mild rebuke to the classical (another example of a *pluriel classique,* for example) but a massive onslaught on French literary tradition.

Rameau is the refugee from the theater fairgrounds who has entered the gilded precincts of grand opera. He has studied its markings, learned its rules and, in an act of comic abandon, set this old-fashioned libretto to music. His action is a profaning of tradition. It is also a death dance for a culture which has lost its bearings, hardened into cliché and thus made itself an ideal target for parody—a form which thrives on identifying dead forms and in submitting them to ridicule.

∞   ∞   ∞

With the demolishing of French classicism through the scene of *l'homme orchestre* an exorcism takes place. A stage has been cleared of impediments which held back various natural forces waiting in the wings for an appropriate moment of disclosure. The Café de la Régence, the makeshift theater where these developments have occurred has become what Peter Brook has called an "empty space."[30]

Diderot's way of introducing these new principles follows the requirements of the *piano à rubans* (and to no small extent the demands of mime). He concentrates them on a single actor or performer. The actor is, of course, Lui. The latter's art is not an instance of clowning or buffoonery at all. It highlights the instant of transcendence vital to the literature of eighteenth-century France; and which gives it a quality of passion out of place only to those who would see the period as the province of "encyclopedists" alone.

Lui's experience has allowed him to shed the dualities of self and society, present and past, which imprisoned him in the categories of civilization. In mime he has tapped a more unified and immediate world of nature, savoured the first state of being, as Rousseau was to call it, which occurs when the shell of culture cracks and a true state of existence comes to the surface in a blinding instant of revelation.

The full script of nature is emblazoned on Rameau as though part of a miraculous process of tattooing or body writing. The sum of human emotion from laughter to grief, silence to delirium is portrayed in his movements and facial gestures. All aesthetic forms and styles, from music, singing and dancing, have broken away from their hierarchies and have become fused in a single aesthetic genre hitherto unknown in French culture. The genre is the one-man show.

The one-man show is connected to many interests of Diderot, to be sure. The troubador or virtuoso performer is one of them. Like troubadors, Lui is a vagabond poet. His taste is intuitive, unharnassed to city judgment. It reveals a "totalizing" side which Diderot viewed as essential to art. As he was to put it in a passage which in many ways is a companion text to the *homme orchestre* scene, in the unity of the arts can be found the first criterion of beauty: "un sage était autrefois un philosophe, un poète, un musicien. Ces talents ont dégénéré en se séparant."[31]

The *homme orchestre* scene has ties too with the history of aesthetics. It stands at the center of the chapter which describes the way theories of representation began to turn away from the dualities of the mimetic or the neoclassical to validate beliefs of a romantic, or, a term which seems to be coming back into vogue, "pre-romantic" kind. Romanticism denies a split between a first source or origin and aesthetic creation. Its orientation is a "genetic" one. The artist merges with nature, takes on its attributes. He becomes, in moments of special vividness, a kind of seer or participant. The condition is the one which Abrams has spoken of as an open-ended process:

For example, organic growth is an open-ended process, nurturing a sense of the promise of the incomplete, and the glory of the imperfect. Also, as a plant assimilates the most diverse materials of earth and air, so the synthetic power of imagination "reveals itself," in Coleridge's famous phrase, "in the balance or reconciliation of *opposite* or *discordant* qualities." And only in a "mechanical" unity are the parts sharply defined and fixed; in organic unity, what we find is a complex inter-relation of living, indeterminate, and endlessly changing components.[32]

The more significant point raised by the *homme orchestre* scene bears, of course, on *spectacle,* the key problematic of Diderot's work. In this scene may be found an answer to the conundrum raised by mime. It is lyrical theater: "criant, chantant, se demenant comme un forcené, faisant a lui seul, les danseurs, les danseuses, les chanteurs, les chanteuses, tout un orchestre, tout un *theatre lyrique.*"

Lyric theater shuns French classical tragedy, the unconscious model or point of reference, as Georges May has observed in *Le Dilemme du roman au dix-huitième siècle,* [33] for all major fictional writings of the time. Tragedy is a depleted form, exhausted of strength, and well-deserving of being reduced to the bits of discourse satirized in the *homme orchestre* scene.

Nor does Diderot's vision of theater endorse the strategies of Rousseau, that figure whose shadow lies over so many pages of the work: in statements about music seemingly lifted word for word from *La Lettre sur la musique française* or *Le Dictionnaire de musique,* autobiographical reminiscences about days spent together in cafés or the astonishing (and surely not coincidental) assonance of Rameau and Rousseau.[34] For Rousseau's conception of theater is a pastoral one, indebted to an *idylle* or village *Fête,* where people take part in what Starobinski has called a milieu of "transparency and nature."[35]

Diderot's *spectacle* endorses the primitive aesthetic called for in his early writings. It is theater as a dionysian experience at whose center is music. Music rids "le vécu de ses entraves, de ses allures maniérées." It conveys what Snyders has termed, in a fundamental contribution to the aesthetics of the *philosophes,* "le jaillissement de la nature."

The text of *l'homme orchestre* is rocked by currents of frenzy and silence, spoken discourse and pantomime alternating with little regard for intelligibility.[36] Its syntax is broken and tumultuous, symbolic of a moment when a civilized model has been dissolved and a new order of passion has burst forth. Nor is the passage designed to be read or studied. It is to be drunk in, impressed on retinas that have been dulled by exposure to tradition.

The passage emphasizes, in a word, the higher lyricism to which the Diderot of the period was drawn.[37] It is *la voix de la nature* perceived as the unsayable or *tremendum*. As such, it is received in the sole manner appropriate to poetic revelation. The manner is one of stunned disbelief, shock, a silence at the furthest remove from "les petits battements de mains."[38]

Rameau, one can thus say, is a *souffleur* or town crier who has come from outside Paris to remind music-goers and critics that nature and lyricism are not dead: "Je descends apparemment en droite ligne du fameux Stentor," he says. And Moi adds, "pour me donner une juste idée de la force de ce viscere, il se mit à tousser d'une violence a ebranler les vitres du caffé, et a suspendre l'attention des joueurs d'echecs."[39]

With his appearance the reversal promised by Socratic comedy does indeed come about. A denial of the body or *ascèse* is changed into a celebration of the physical. Discourse of an ecstatic kind replaces *l'écriture classique*. Music assumes priority over literature. Diderot even has Rameau throw out the condition which is regarded as the *sine qua non* of theatrical experience. The condition is community.

Classical theater takes place in a public space. It portrays myths of a communal kind. Viewers or spectators are required. And a given performance is conceived less as a mere entertainment or diversion than a catharsis. Tragedy purges hubris; comedy levels low vanity and *méprise*. In these activities may be found the source of a potential reintegration of self and society.

Rameau's art takes place outside this civilized framework. It is solipsistic. Herein, of course, lies its originality. For Rameau has transcended society. He has tapped the new absolute of nature and in so doing created a theater of self (or *Fête solitaire*). The discovery could not be more radical. For it empties out Rousseau's *Le Devin du village* and the pages of

La Lettre à d'Alembert devoted to the festivals and pageants of small Swiss mountain villages. With the unveiling of the one-man show, European dramatic theater leaves the eighteenth century. It is now directed at totalizing productions of the century to come.

IV

Anti-Theater

THAT THIS RECOVERY OF NATURE will be short-lived will not surprise readers of eighteenth-century French literature. All literary works of the period which evoke natural *présence* or transcendence (and, as suggested, they are far more numerous than generally perceived) do so in an ironic manner.

Once a breakthrough to a first ground of being has been achieved, ways are found of backing away from such a discovery, placing the integrity of nature into question, and, as a result, centering a text on a dual or ironic structure best described by Jean Starobinski as "la transparence et l'obstacle."[1]

Language provides one example of this duality. Though Diderot's story speaks of a state of being outside literary discourse (or even in scenes like *l'homme orchestre* a condition impervious to human speech), it cannot grant such a condition permanent form. Recourse to language or written signs is inevitable. Only through the description of Lui's art can the full extent of his "baptism in nature" be recorded. The narrator performs this role. He comments on the shock produced by Lui's appearance and, to no small extent, his own collapse in face of it.

Fiction supplies a second mode of distancing from nature. Moi's claims to the contrary, he did not actually meet Lui at the Café de la Régence, become involved with him in discussions about opera, and the music lesson which brought him to his knees. His encounter was an imaginary event. One is to take it as a dream sequence. It stages a "transcendence" by a musical beggar. Like all fictional tales, it is inseparable from illusions and tricks. Among them are, as already noted, plays of perspective, blurred time schemes and a narrative presence split into two competing voices.

As is so often the case in eighteenth-century narratives whose background is nature or transcendence, time also plays a crucial role. At issue here is a gap between two states of existence. The first is indeed an instant of bliss or ecstasy. The second is the illumination understood as having already taken place, been located in the past, and as a result seen as a source of nostalgia and regret.

In making use of these ironies, Diderot seems to have picked up the trail of Rousseau once again. For it is in the writings of this *philosophe* (or *anti-philosophe*) that the tensions between transcendence and reality, nature and literature achieve exemplary formulation both as a meditation on romantic belief and, as de Man has suggested, a way of stating the problem of the "blindness and insight" of writing.[2]

Many of Rousseau's works reflect these concerns, from the early essay on language entitled *L'Essai sur l'origine des langues* to later writings like *La Nouvelle Héloïse* and *Les Confessions*. But Rousseau's conception of "supplementarity" is nowhere more apparent, or expressed with greater force, than in a short work conceived toward the end of his life. This text is *Les Rêveries du promeneur solitaire*. The writing has come to be thought of as a lost chapter to the *Confessions*.

"Rousseau" is the main character of this work and the fifth *Rêverie* the central section. This chapter describes Rousseau's withdrawal to the Island of Saint Peter. Here he finds a retreat from the treacheries of Parisians and the stoning in Môtiers. He reclines in a boat on a remote mountain lake, enjoys the peace of a part of Switzerland as yet unsullied by "stocking factories" and becomes alive to the pleasures of what he calls *le romantique*—a word used for the first time in French literature, as Marcel Raymond has pointed out, with the associations and connotations now taken for granted.[3]

Soon nature takes over. Rousseau's consciousness dissolves like the water around him. He loses all sense of self. The dualities of nature and culture, selfhood and community, which made him a prisoner of categories of philosophy or history are peeled away. He can now savour the bliss of an oceanic first state of being:

> Mais s'il est un état où l'ame trouve une assiete assez solide pour s'y reposer tout entière et rassembler là tout son être, sans avoir besoin de rappeller le passé ni d'enjamber sur l'avenir; où le tems ne soit rien pour elle, où le présent dure toujours sans neanmoins marquer sa durée et sans aucune trace de succession, sans aucun autre sentiment de privation ni de jouissance, de plaisir ni de peine, de désir ni de crainte que celui seul de notre existence, et que ce sentiment seul puisse la remplir tout entière; tant que cet état dure celui qui s'y trouve peut s'appeller heureux, non d'un bonheur imparfait, pauvre et relatif tel que celui qu'on trouve dans les plaisirs de la vie mais d'un bonheur suffisant, parfait et plein, qui ne laisse dans l'âme aucun vuide qu'elle sente le besoin de remplir. Tel est l'état où je me suis trouvé souvent à l'Isle de St Pierre dans mes reveries solitaires, soit couché dans mon bateau que je laissois dériver au gré de l'eau, soit assis sur les rives du lac agité, soit ailleurs au bord d'une belle rivière ou d'un ruisseau murmurant sur le gravier.[4]

Rousseau refers to this moment as an ecstatic one, outside history. He expresses the wish that such a *ravissement* (as he also calls it) could last forever:

> Tout est dans un flux continuel sur la terre. Rien n'y garde une forme constante et arrêtée, et nos affections qui s'attachent aux choses extérieures passent et changent necessairement comme elles. Toujours en avant ou en arrière de nous, elles rappellent le passé qui n'est plus ou previennent l'avenir qui souvent ne doit point être: il n'y a rien là de solide à quoi le cœur se puisse attacher. Aussi n'a-t-on guère ici bas que du plaisir qui passe; pour le bonheur qui dure je doute qu'il y soit connu. A peine est-il dans nos plus vives jouissances un instant où le cœur puisse véritablement nous dire! Je voudrais que cet instant durât toujours; et comment peut-on appeler bonheur un état fugitif qui nous laisse encor le cœur inquiet et vuide, qui nous fait regretter quelque chose avant, ou désirer encore quelque chose après?[5]

But of course it cannot. As Grimsley has observed, moments of this kind have no binding force. "It is important to recall," he states, "that the perfect *rêverie* described in the fifth *promenade* is, in fact, a memory of a previous emotional experience which may have been idealized and embellished through the process of later self-reflection. In a sense, therefore, the *rêverie* of the Ile de Saint-Pierre remains an imaginative possibility which was never experienced in exactly the same way as Rousseau describes it; it is a recreation of the past rather than the concrete reality of the present."[6]

Rousseau uses a key image to express this loss of nature. It is the herbarium or *herbier*:

> Toutes mes courses de botanique, les diverses impressions du local des objets qui m'ont frappé, les idées qu'il m'a fait naître, les incidens qui s'y sont mêlés, tout cela m'a laissé des impressions qui se renouvellent par l'aspect des plantes herborisées dans ces mêmes lieux. Je ne reverrai plus ces beaux paysages, ces forêts, ces lacs, ces bosquets, ces rochers, ces montagnes dont l'aspect a toujours touché mon cœur: mais maintenant que je ne peux plus courir ces heureuses contrées je n'ai qu'à ouvrir mon herbier et bientot il m'y transporte. Les fragmens des plantes que j'y ai cueillies suffisent pour me rappeler tout ce magnifique spectacle. Cet herbier est pour moi un journal d'herborisations qui me les fait recommencer avec un nouveau charme et produit l'effet d'une optique qui les peindroit derechef à mes yeux.
>
> C'est la chaîne des idées accessoires qui m'attache à la botanique. Elle rassemble et rappelle à mon imagination toutes les idées qui la flatent davantage. Les prés, les eaux, les bois, la solitude, la paix surtout et le repos qu'on trouve au milieu de tout cela sont retracés par elle incessamment à ma mémoire. Elle me fait oublier les persécutions des hommes, leur haine, leur mépris, leurs outrages, et tous les maux dont ils ont payé mon tendre et sincère attachement pour eux. Elle me transporte dans des habitations paisibles au milieu de gens simples et bons, tels que ceux avec qui j'ai vécu jadis. Elle me rappelle et mon jeune âge et mes innocents plaisirs, elle m'en fait jouir derechef, et me rend heureux bien souvent encore au milieu du plus triste sort qu'ait subi jamais un mortel.[7]

The *herbier* is a double book. On the one hand, it is a magic volume containing leaves from plants like the *dentaire heptaphyllos, ciclamen, nidus avis, lacerpodious,* and other flowers of the *Flora Petrinsularis*.[8] These plants evoke the beauty of nature unsullied by vain systematizing or ambition. Flowers embody youth, innocence, the purity of tramps in the Swiss countryside. The book in which they have been pressed is indeed a *livre de la nature.* Its presence cancels out those other texts which Rousseau calls "les tristes paperasses" or "la bouquinerie."[9]

On the other hand, though, the *herbier* is an artifact of literature. It bears witness to a desire to embalm nature in a cultural document and to dramatize a loss of transcendence rather than its recovery. The purity of time past can only be recovered or brought back to life when the pages of the *herbier* are turned by an act of *will*. Only then can nature reappear as though by command (a situation which, some scholars have said, represents the status of literature in general). The latter is an area of creation which can never fuse with its subject. Its success requires the "poison" of language.

Yet just as Diderot revises the pastoral qualities of Rousseau into the frenzy of *l'homme orchestre* or in his work deepens satiric thrusts found only in occasional chapters in Rousseau (the Parisian scenes, for example, of *La Nouvelle Héloïse)* into an œuvre dictated by satire, so too does he take his distance from his former friend on the issue of irony and transcendence.

His work contains a mode of irony unknown in Rousseau, indeed deeply hostile to it. The mode is comic travesty: the portrayal of nature in a grotesque and debased manner. The point of such travesty is simple enough. It is to reject the balance and moderation of traditional comedy. Diderot's stance will be a more ruthless and absolute one. Comedy will emphasize conflict and discord. It will bring to the story of Lui and Moi a mood always avoided in *facéties*. The mood is one of emptiness and despair.[10]

∞   ∞   ∞

Lui is crucial to this travesty. With the end of the ecstatic moment of nature, he is thrown back on his former condition as bohemian oddity or outcast. The narrator is especially clear on this point. In the comments appended to the last pages of the scene, he describes a performer who gasps for breath, reverts to earlier discussions about philosophy and ethics and—a highly significant change whose importance is more apparent when *Rameau's Nephew* is staged as a play—uses the kind of spoken French which offers a stunning contrast—even rejection—of the silence that preceded it:

> Tandis qu'il me parloit ainsi, la foule qui nous environnoit, ou n'entendant rien ou prenant peu d'interet a ce qu'il disoit, parce qu'en general l'enfant comme l'homme, et l'homme comme l'enfant aime mieux s'amuser que s'instruire, s'etoit retirée; chacun etoit a son jeu; et nous etions restés seuls dans notre coin. Assis sur une banquette, la tete appuyee contre le mur, les bras pendants, les yeux a demi fermés, il me dit: je ne scais ce que j'ai; quand je suis venu ici, j'etois frais et dispos, et me voila roué, brisé comme si j'avois fait dix lieues. Cela m'a pris subitement.
> Moi.-Voulez vous vous rafraichir?
> Lui.-Volontiers. Je me sens enroué. Les forces me manquent; et je souffre un peu de la poitrine. Cela m'arrive presque tous les jours, comme cela; sans que je sache pourquoi.[11]

Pantomime is essential to Lui's art, to be sure. It is the single non-literary influence of *Le Neveu de Rameau* whose potential is constantly developed and broadened in Diderot's text. Mime now probes into a subject connected with the end of transcendence. The subject is Lui's own consciousness, portrayed through the tensions and ambiguities of those who live in two worlds.

On the one hand, Lui's mime draws attention to his social standing in the Paris of the mid-1750s. The condition is that of a street musician or, as he says in a not unusual confidence or aside, a "misérable racleur de cordes:"

> Oui, quand on excelle; mais qui est ce qui peut se promettre de son enfant qu'il excellera? Il y a dix mille a parler contre un qu'il ne seroit qu'un miserable racleur de cordes, comme moi. Scavez vous qu'il seroit peut etre plus aisé de trouver un enfant propre a gouverner un royaume, a faire un grand roi qu'un grand violon.[12]

Fate, or *la molécule paternelle,* has condemned the "nephew of Rameau" to poverty, ostracism, and the occasional musical lesson at the house of wealthy patrons (the latter described with a pacing and comic relief worthy of some of the best scenes in Molière or Goldoni). His existence follows the cycle of despair and success caused by Vertumnis. But it is also governed by historical reality. For musicians in eighteenth-century France could well have, as Rameau says, spent their Mondays at a table of elegant bankers, and their Wednesdays skulking about Paris, looking for handouts with the dejected mien which would make one think that they had indeed just come from a long stay with the Trappists:

> Rien ne dissemble plus de lui que lui meme. Quelquefois, il est maigre et have, comme un malade au dernier degré de la consomption; on compteroit ses dents a travers ses joues; on diroit qu'il a passé plusieurs jours sans manger, ou qu'il sort de la Trape. Le mois suivant, il est gras et replet, comme s'il n'avoit pas quitté la table d'un financier, ou qu'il eut été renfermé dans un couvent de Bernardins.[13]

Yet Lui is not entirely pinioned in this role. Moments of high creation like *l'homme orchestre* scene allow him to transcend his empirical status. Through mime, Lui can create roles immune to history. Here he dramatizes potential states of being. They are, like the hermaphrodite, outside passport identity, held in check only by the force of imagination.

Nor does mime seek to synthesize these warring states. It is an existential art rather than a stable one. Mime dramatizes a fissure in self or lack of being. It allows Rameau to juggle the conflicting sides of himself in the air, to hold them up before the *badauds* who come to gaze at him much as they would at any free public spectacle and to state the claims of a new belief at once empty and fulfilled, sublime and debased—one which has broken with the traditions of Molière and Voltaire. The belief is a *cogito du vide*.[14]

Lui's art disdains, for example, the mask. The latter is a traditional prop of comic theater. It certifies that what is being staged is an illusion meant to restore the order of society when the curtain falls. At such a time, true identities will be revealed, false confidences explained, and the stable foundation of being momentarily turned upside down in comedy, restored and celebrated (more often than not through a shared public event like marriage).[15]

Rameau's use of masks is more open-ended. One is to take it as an example of what Bakhtin was to call "romantic disguise":

> In its Romantic form the mask is torn away from the oneness of the folk carnival concept. It is stripped of its original richness and acquires other meanings alien to its primitive nature; now the mask hides sometimes, keeps a secret, deceives. Such a meaning would not be possible as long as the mask functioned within folk culture's organic whole. The Romantic mask loses almost entirely its regenerating and renewing element and acquires a somber hue. A terrible vacuum, a nothingness lurks behind it. (This theme is strikingly presented in Bonaventura's "Night Watches.") But an inexhaustible and many-colored life can always be described behind the mask of folk grotesque.[16]

Mime encourages an unusual kind of comic invention as well, one far removed from the simple upside-down ploys of the Saturnalia or other *folles journées*. For Lui's mime is openly nihilistic. It involves the individual in a process of invention meant to unravel the self, deny it a center of identity, ultimately indeed to bring into play the kind of endless reduplication, even madness, often seen in exercises of the kind (*Rousseau juge de Jean-Jacques,* for example).[17]

Mime even subverts the fundamental assumption of comic acting. It is that performances like *l'homme orchestre* ought to lead to moral instruction and the kind of laughter or release in which, as Baudelaire was to observe in his great essay on comedy, lies the essence of French wit: "En France, pays de pensée et de démonstration claires, où l'art vise naturellement et directement à l'utilité, le comique est généralement significatif."[18]

What mime emphasizes rather is a darker kind of humor. It is comedy as related to the "absolute laughter" Baudelaire reported on in his visit to a troupe of English acrobats and mimes:

> Je garderai longtemps le souvenir de la première pantomime anglaise que j'aie vu jouer. C'était au théâtre des Variétés, il y a quelques années. Peu de gens s'en souviendront sans doute, car bien peu ont paru goûter ce genre de divertissement, et ces pauvres mimes anglais reçurent chez nous un triste accueil. Le public français n'aime guère être dépaysé. Il n'a pas le goût très-cosmopolite, et les déplacements d'horizon lui troublent la vue. Pour mon compte, je fus excessivement frappé de cette manière de comprendre le comique. On disait, et

> c'étaient les indulgents, pour expliquer l'insuccès, que c'étaient des artistes vulgaires et médiocres, des doublures; mais ce n'était pas là la question. Ils étaient Anglais, c'est là l'important.
>
> Il m'a semblé que le signe distinctif de ce genre de comique était la violence. Je vais en donner la preuve par quelques échantillons de mes souvenirs.
>
> D'abord, le Pierrot n'était pas ce personnage pâle comme la lune, mystérieux comme le silence, souple et muet comme le serpent, droit et long comme une potence, cet homme artificiel, mû par des ressorts singuliers, auquel nous avait accoutumés le regrettable Debureau. Le Pierrot anglais arrivait comme la tempête, tombait comme un ballot, et quand il riait, son rire faisait trembler la salle; ce rire ressemblait à un joyeux tonnerre. C'était un homme court et gros, ayant augmenté sa préstance par un costume chargé de rubans, qui faisaient autour de sa jubilante personne l'office des plumes et du duvet autour des oiseaux, ou de la fourrure autour des angoras. Par-dessus la farine de son visage, il avait collé crûment, sans gradation, sans transition, deux énormes plaques de rouge pur. La bouche était agrandie par une prolongation simulée des lèvres au moyen de deux bandes de carmin, de sorte que, quand il riait, la gueule avait l'air de courir jusqu'aux oreilles.[19]

The subject of comedy, that is to say, is the fallen self rather than the social one. Its vision is not the poise of art (or language) but the gratuitousness of existence. And the reaction called for by this strange exhibition of self is not catharsis at all. The desired effect of mime is discomfiture, uneasiness, a kind of metallic grimace.

∞   ∞   ∞

Other parts of Diderot's story pick up this mood of debased caricature, much as they did the overture passage. Narrative description is one of them. It displays an interest in crude detail hardly consonant with Horatian satire. The latter is indeed a "low" form. Yet it inevitably purifies vulgarity through fantasy and comic indulgence. One finds in *Le Neveu de Rameau* low detail of a more concerted and autonomous kind. Its links are not so much with satire as with contemporary novels like *La Vie de*

Marianne (the coachman scene) or *Manon Lescaut* (the passage about convicts and prison ships).

The first few pages of the book introduce the theme. Here the narrator speaks of taverns on the outer reaches of the city where hustlers and social parasites come to meet: "ou il regagne, a pié, un petit grenier qu'il habite, a moins que l'hotesse ennuyée d'attendre son loyer, ne lui en ait redemandé la clef; ou il se rabbat dans une taverne du faubourg ou il attend le jour, entre un morceau de pain et un pot de bierre."[20] The reader learns of derelicts who sleep in coach houses and wake up in the morning with straw in their hair and the smell of horses permeating their clothes: "Quand il n'a pas six sols dans sa poche, ce qui lui arrive quelquefois, il a recours soit a un fiacre de ses amis, soit au cocher d'un grand seigneur qui lui donne un lit sur de la paille, a coté de ses chevaux. Le matin, il a encore une partie de son matelas dans ses cheveux;" "Au lieu d'un sommeil doux et tranquille, comme vous l'aviez, vous entendrez d'une oreille le hennissement et le pietinement des chevaux, de l'autre, le bruit mille fois plus insupportable des vers secs, durs et barbares."[21] There is, as well, a highly developed sense of the poetry of the city of Paris when night falls and the streets have been abandoned by honest citizens and taken over by prowlers and criminals. "La nuit amene aussi son inquietude,"[22] writes the narrator—a sentence which can be read both as a reminder of Lui's anxious condition and as a foreshadowing of a new interest in the metropolis and its "encroaching vastness."[23]

The story shows a concern too with language of an extraordinarily trivialized and stricken kind. "Billingsgate," a term used by Bakhtin, best describes the idiom. It seeks to debunk official culture or principles of "an unmoving and unchanging hierarchy in which the higher and the lower never merge."[24] What language now shows is the vitality and freshness of popular discourse and morality.

"Tout ce qui vit, sans l'en excepter, cherche son bien etre au depens d'autrui;" "Nous paroissons gais, mais au fond nous avons tous de l'humeur et grand appetit. Des loups ne sont pas plus affamés, des tigres ne sont pas plus cruels. Nous devorons comme des loups, lors que la terre a eté longtemps couverte de neige; nous dechirons comme des tigres tout ce qui reussit." These are the maxims needed to survive in the world, says Lui. They are filled out with the crude hedonism of "drinking fine vintages, gorging oneself with delicacies, rolling on pretty women, sleeping in soft linen;" and—the final arbiter of matters of conscience—innards and guts ("la tribulation des intestins").[25]

As is typical of many a story in Diderot, *Rameau's Nephew* also exploits the grotesque. But the idiom used in the story of Lui and Moi is a far cry from the comic exuberance of *Jacques le fataliste,* where executioners, gallows, *fourches patibulaires,* coffins, and, as the narrator says in a celebrated passage, a funeral cortege accompanied by "un char drapé de noir, traîné par quatre chevaux noirs, couverts de housses noires qui leur enveloppaient la tête et qui descendaient jusqu'à leurs pieds; derrière, deux domestiques en noir; à la suite deux autres vêtus de noir, chacun sur un cheval noir, caparaçonné de noir; sur le siège du char un cocher noir, le chapeau rabattu et entouré d'un long crêpe qui pendait le long de son épaule gauche" come together in a buoyant hymn to the dissolution of form and Shandian irony.[26]

What prevails in *Le Neveu de Rameau* is a more melancholy idiom. Its kinship is with the "agonized" vein of grotesque writing spoken of by Mario Praz in *The Romantic Agony;* or a "gothic" streak already visible in such episodes of *La Religieuse* as the prison scene ("on ouvrait avec de grosses clefs la porte d'un petit lieu souterrain, obscur, où l'on me jeta sur une natte que l'humidité avait à demi pourrie. Là, je trouvai un morceau de pain noir et une cruche d'eau avec quelques vaisseaux nécessaires et grossiers. La natte roulée par un bout formait un oreiller; il y avait sur un bloc de pierre, une tête de mort, avec un crucifix de bois"); or Suzanne's macabre night initiation: "A la fin de l'office, on me fit coucher dans une bière au milieu du chœur; on plaça des chandeliers à mes côtés, avec un bénitier; on me couvrit d'un suaire, et l'on récita l'office des morts, après lequel chaque religieuse, en sortant, me jeta de l'eau bénite en disant: Requiescat in pace".[27]

Ugliness and physical disability contribute to this mood:

> Et puis voux voyez bien ce poignet; il etait roide comme un diable. Ces dix doigts, c'etoient autant de batons fichés dans un metacarpe de bois; et ces tendons, c'etoient de vieilles cordes a boyaux plus seches, plus roides, plus inflexibles que celles qui ont servi a la roue d'un tourneur. Mais je vous les ai tant tourmentées, tant brisées, tant

rompues. Tu ne veux pas aller; et moi, mordieu, je dis que tu iras, et cela sera.[28]

"Worm-like" positions are emphasized. "L'allure du ver, c'est mon allure," Lui says.[29] Diderot's narrator refers also to young provincials imprudent enough to have put their arm through a tiger's cage at the Versailles zoo and to have left it behind.

The central part of the grotesque idiom, never far from conversations about music or philosophy, is death. Here, as both Kayser and Bakhtin have observed, lies the essence of the grotesque: "Pourir sous du marbre, pourir sous de la terre, c'est toujours pourir. Avoir autour de son cercueil les enfants rouges et les enfants bleus, ou n'avoir personne, qu'est-ce que cela fait." The phrase, already compelling in its evocation of the vanity of life, is filled out by a reference to the obsequies of a rich banker:

> Au dernier moment tous sont egalement riches; et Samuel Bernard qui a force de vols, de pillages, de banqueroutes laisse vingt sept millions en or, et Rameau qui ne laissera rien; Rameau a qui la charité fournira la serpilliere dont on l'enveloppera. La mort n'entend pas sonner les cloches. C'est en vain que cent prêtres s'egosillent pour lui: qu'il est precedé et suivi d'une longue file de torches ardentes; son ame ne marche pas a coté du maitre des ceremonies.[30]

∞ ∞ ∞

These low details force on Diderot's story many curious interests, the more striking because of the unexpected way they are presented and the contrast they establish with the bantering tone on which *Le Neveu de Rameau* began.

The inequity of class is one of them. In this theme lies the source of much speculation on motive and psychology, from the outbursts of Figaro against those who "merely took the trouble to be born" to discussions of servants in the *Confessions* and many a tiff between master and servant in *Jacques le fataliste*. Mime, a murky art at best, gives shape to these feelings of *ressentiment*. It expresses the claims of outcasts and marginals on whose behalf Lui speaks and whose lack of culture and social acceptance serves in some paradoxical way as proof of their high status.

Mime is also violent. It breathes the spirit of rebellion of various Pirate Jennies and the schemes of revenge they dream of putting into action when they will no longer be flunkies but in charge. Then they will administer justice to their former oppressors. "What would you do," Moi asks Lui, "if you ever became rich?" The answer is startling in its frankness and brutality:

> Je ferois comme tous les gueux revetus; je serois le plus insolent maroufle qu'on eut encore vu. C'est alors que je me rappellerois tout ce qu'ils m'ont fait souffrir; et je leur rendrois bien les avanies qu'ils m'ont faites. J'aime a commander, et je commanderai. J'aime qu'on me loue et l'on me louera. J'aurai a mes gages, toute la troupe vilmorienne, et je leur dirai, comme on me l'a dit, Allons, faquins, qu'on m'amuse et l'on m'amusera; qu'on me dechire les honnetes gens, et on les dechirera....[31]

The low features of *Le Neveu de Rameau* suggest affinities with history as well. They point up the discovery, through mime and language, of a region of France as exotic to contemporary readers of *Le Neveu de Rameau* as the Tahiti of *Le Supplément au voyage de Bougainville*. The region is Paris: a city lying under the eyes of Diderot's audience but whose importance they have yet to recognize.

Nor is the Paris of Diderot's story the comfortable space of the Palais Royal and the banc d'Argenson where Moi and other dilettante scholars would go for a stroll and enjoy the amusing sights open to the *flâneur*. This tiny aristocratic Paris has been broken open and replaced by the city crouching in the interstices of Diderot's text. It is the nascent metropolis of the late eighteenth and early nineteenth centuries.

Here may be found the *faubourg* (a term specifically used by the narrator). Paris is the breeding place of outcasts and marginals familiar to Rameau. The city is the haunt too of that other "character" whose appearance in an eighteenth-century satire gives it a strikingly modern tone. This character is the *foule* or urban crowd: the silent chorus to the great scene of Lui's pantomime (and of course a faceless one).

The more permanent meaning of these low currents bears on the games of irony and self-parody in which lie a dominant interest of the story. One point is essential in this regard. References to *ressentiment* or a second Paris are not isolated or accidental. They form a fully worked out structure of a hidden or underground kind. This structure dramatizes another ironic twist or *dédoublement*. It tells the story of the *Fête* or pageant of nature in a debased and fallen way.

∞ ∞ ∞

Rameau, as now seems clear, is the troubadour of nature who has, with the end of the one-man show, been stripped of his mythical status and reduced to the condition of a *real homme orchestre* or one-man band. Performers of this kind crowded the streets of eighteenth-century Paris. They congregated, more often than not, near the Pont Neuf. The description Mercier provides of one such minstrel or street entertainer is strikingly reminiscent of Lui:

> A harmonica would dangle from the mouth of this musician and rest on a stand tucked into his belt. A string hung from his left arm on which was attached a drumstick-affair that would, when rattled, strike a bass-drum. A long suspender device went round his torso and held a triangle. The *homme orchestre* wore boots to which cymbals were attached and played them by clicking his heels. He also had a banjo. The performance was perfectly calibrated so that at the slightest movement the whole thing would go off like a musical fire alarm.[32]

There were indeed many other *Orphées ambulants,* as they were called, who could imitate Rameau's art and show how widespread it was: the Savoyard, for instance, known as the Orpheus of the Pont Neuf, whose voice could be heard from the Louvre to the Rue Dauphine; the idiot boy who claimed to be Orlando Lasso; Apollon de la Grève, a blind violinist accompanied by a woman with a bagpipe; Louis the organist with his hideous face and long dress; and countless other members of the same "fraternity of street singers."[33]

Pantomime, the great art form of *Le Neveu de Rameau*, sheds its style of broad farce, or what Lui was to call the art of *la grosse bête*. It endorses a higher clowning of a metaphysical kind. Mime provides a portrait of the artist as buffoon or failed Pierrot (a favored way, of course, of allowing artists to stage a drama of their own isolation and exile).[34]

Discourse retreats from the witticisms of Voltaire or Horace. It adopts a tone whose imaginative energy derives from an aesthetic of "cruelty." Cruel writings do indeed mock the folly of philosophy. They also turn satire on itself and show the vanity of writing and literature.[35]

Even the Café de la Régence, the unlikely vehicle for Rameau's initiation is overthrown. After the failure of the ecstatic instant it can no longer be taken as a magic stage or return to the open-air theaters of classical antiquity. The Café de la Régence is merely a place people go to when they are bored, "le refuge des oisifs," as the narrator says, explaining his reasons for going there in the first place. Its address is all too well known and common: a few doors down from the Palais Royal.[36]

With the fall of this last bastion of nature, Diderot's entire drama of nature collapses. What Lui's performance symbolizes is not the coming of nature or *la Fête*. It is the failure of nature: the return to what Rousseau was to call *divertissement*.

No one literary reference conveys the force of this anti-theater, though several come to mind as possibilities. *The Beggar's Opera* is one of them.[37] Gay's work shares many interests in outcast philosophy and parody of contemporary musical themes. Urban pastoral (the phrase of Empson) is another.[38] So, too, is what Starobinski was to call the "Pageant Denied."

Yet whatever term is ultimately selected, there can be little doubt as to the essence of such a performance or the condition it validates. It is the replacement of *La Fête* and the ecstatic moment with the banalities of history and the conscious self:

> La fête heureuse proclame l'union des cœurs; l'inspiration profonde atteste l'unité du génie et de la nature. Ne pourrait-on rêver d'une plus haute synthèse, où la fête et le génie, où l'unité sociale et l'immédiate présence de la nature seraient confondus? Le désir de la suprême unité hante quelques grandes œuvres littéraires—celles de Rousseau et de Hœlderlin—mais ne s'y manifeste que pour aboutir au constat de

> l'impossible: plus exaltante aura été l'image de l'unité visée, plus tragique le destin qui foudroie ceux qui l'ont conçue.³⁹

La roue de fortune best catches the spirit of this shift.⁴⁰ The reference is a carnival one, to be sure. It is used by Lui at the end of his meeting with Moi. At this point, though, carnival no longer symbolizes the Saturnalia. Its focus is popular theater of a more modern and disturbing kind, whose point is to show nature as arbitrary and hollow.

The calendar of Parisian entertainments, in other words, did not come to an end with the moment of Rameau's appearance at the Café de la Régence. It only appeared to do so. With the conclusion of Lui's brief role as "dionysian poet," the old ways of society and literature assert themselves anew; and with the power that comes from law. The *homme orchestre* scene was at best an exercise in false consciousness and illusion.

V
Satyre 2de

AS BROUGHT TO THIS POINT IN OUR STUDY, *Rameau's Nephew* resembles the curiosity Horace satirized in the *Ars Poetica* when he spoke about an artist who joined a human head to the neck of a horse, spread colored feathers over limbs picked up at random, and created an oddity whose top was a beautiful female and whose bottom a black and ugly fish.[1]

Diderot's narrative blends philosophical dialogue, autobiography, and a wide variety of ironic *dédoublements* and masks. Time patterns shift back and forth between myth, the ecstatic moment and the fallen temporality of the wheel of fortune. Comic techniques mix Voltairian farce, *commedia dell'arte* and the new subjective clown routines administered by Rameau to himself. And the structure of *Le Neveu de Rameau* pushes *mélange*—the ruling principle of satire—to a compound of pantomime and writing, music and ballet, unrecognized by any previous comic form.

It is at this moment where the story of Lui and Moi appears to have plunged into a spiral not unlike some of the more extravagant routines of Lui that the second reading always present in a Diderot narrative emerges. The reading is governed by a critical strain which informs all his works, however eccentric or unruly their outer form. At their center is one technique. It is self-parody.

The oddities and contradictions mentioned above reflect self-parody. They indicate the reality of a literary work which has abandoned the comforts of traditional writing (or ways of speaking about literature) for the more strenuous requirements of a "text." Texts call into question the genre in which they were written. They use the ironies of narration to which such an enterprise inevitably leads as a novel subject of a negative kind and as a formal structure as well.

Parody is, of course, a staple of Enlightenment fiction. One finds it in narratives from *Candide* (a take-off on *Quixote* and novels of chivalry) to *Justine* (a burlesque re-writing of *La Nouvelle Héloïse*). Yet Diderot's use of parody could not be more different from that of his great philosophical relatives.

For Diderot's work does not strive to provide an example of the hollowness or inadequacy of fiction: a form split between the higher knowledge of the storyteller, a calm patrician voice speculating in the comfort of his study on the folly of the world, and the ignorance of the *naïfs* he writes about (characters whose absurdity forecloses any maturing or growth and underscores the vanity of the philosophical quest on which they embarked).

Diderot's stories mine a more constructive and self-aware vein of parody. If parody does indeed dramatize the failure of a given genre, it also encourages critical contrast and growth. Parody is inseparable, as Tynianov has written, from the existence of "une matière nouvelle qui n'est autre que l'ancien procédé mécanisé." Above all, parody leads to a rewriting of genre which is the result of an enlightened confrontation between old and new, and in which lies a major difference between this mode and pastiche—a comic form with which parody is often confused.[2]

Italian opera is the key to this usage. Far from being an incidental or anecdotal reference, opera supplies the drive and momentum of Diderot's text. Opera gives music, a subject generally neglected by the *philosophes,* or consigned to a ritual visit to a single musical performance *(Les Lettres Persanes)* or a short bantering conversation *(Candide),* unexpected depth and force. Opera sparks the *homme orchestre* scene and the pantomime essential to it. Even more significantly, Diderot's narrator conceives of opera as a Socratic form. It thus possesses special leavening qualities and dialectical force.

Diderot's narrator goes to some lengths to underscore this affinity between opera and the Socratic. It is stated in a general way through common interests in comic dialogue and mime, of course. An interest in satirizing first aesthetic forms (classical French opera and the tragedies of Racine, in the case of Rameau; early Greek tragedy with respect to Socrates) supplies another shared reference. The deeper connection comes through close and numerous references to Socrates himself. They are found throughout the text and point to Lui's status as a kind of Socrates *redivivus*.

If the latter has his *daimon* or irrational voice that tells him what not to do, Rameau is "possessed" by *la maudite molécule paternelle*. Both are ugly. They symbolize a new link between ordinary appearance and extraordinary inner subjective truth. Socrates, we know from many sources, was bald, had a walk like the strut of a fowl, a large nose, and eyes with a prominent space between them that caused his friends to think that he looked like the satyr Marsyas. Rameau's appearance (as shown in the illustration which accompanies the first French edition of the text) is that of a broken-nosed pugilist. His visage, as he says, "caused nature to make a face, and then another face, and then another."[3]

Both are of problematical social origin: Socrates the son of a midwife; Lui the "nephew" of Rameau, lacking in patronymic and, as a consequence, the power to name. A bohemian style of discourse underscores another shared feature. Neither Socrates nor Rameau write treatises or attend meetings of the Academy. Their philosophical office is the street. There they meet strangers (accost them really, *aborder* is the word used by the narrator to describe the way Lui first grabbed hold of Moi) and start dialogue. The latter is not an external process of inquiry or a form of calm exposition. It represents a new kind of communal discussion and dramatization. Through dialogue, first beliefs are broken down and discarded. The listener is "paralyzed" by this method and removed from the hold of tradition. Eventually truth is brought forth.[4] Plato uses the word *maieutic* to describe the phenomenon. In *Rameau's Nephew* the process is referred to as *accouchement:* "C'est cela, je crois. Voila que cela vient; voila ce que c'est que de trouver un accoucheur qui scait irriter, precipiter les douleurs et faire sortir l'enfant...."[5]

The Socratic reference furthers many interests of Diderot, to be sure. A connection with the *parti des philosophes* is one of them. With Socrates, the narrator is able to stage a highly flattering self-portrait of the *philosophes,* if not indeed Diderot himself. Diderot, like his fellow *philosophes,* thought of Socrates as a pagan saint. His martyrdom had exemplary meaning. One was to view him, Peter Gay has observed, as a key member of a collective conscience of the ancients, "whose approval

Diderot sought and whose counsel he feared."[6] As we know from Arthur Wilson's biography of Diderot, the *philosophe* spent a good part of his time in Vincennes prison translating the *Apology*. Diderot's papers speak of a project about the death of Socrates.[7] The *Correspondance* is filled with references to the extraordinary nobility of the man. Remarks on Socrates can be found in many other parts of the *œuvre* as well, both in the *Encyclopédie* and *La Réfutation d'Helvétius*.

The Socratic influence can also be brought back to Rousseau, that shadowy figure who stands behind so many pages of *Rameau's Nephew*. For readers of Diderot's time could well have taken "Lui-Socrates" for the charlatan Rousseau was held to be by many of his contemporaries. Like Socrates, Rousseau shunned orthodox dress. His views on nature and society expressed an interest in the absolute or the romantic which could well have irked audiences already familiar with the differences between Alceste and Philinte. Moreover, the relationship between Diderot and his former friend had, by the time of the writing of *Rameau's Nephew*, deteriorated to the point where a caricature of this kind would not have been considered a violation of their friendship.[8]

The more fundamental Socratic reference pertains, as stated earlier, to the comic ironies in which lie the second or "true" subject of Diderot's narrative. With Socrates a hitherto unknown form of comic irony is brought to bear on Diderot's story. It is dialectics: irony used not only as a means of dramatizing conflict or aporia but as a source of integration and recovery.

A line spoken by Lui serves as an especially revealing introduction to this link between the Socratic and the operatic. It comes in the passage where Lui speaks of the way Italian music knocked the old idols of France out of their sockets and submitted them to the shock of the new:

> Ma foi, ces maudits bouffons, avec leur *Servante maitresse*, leur *Tracollo*, nous en ont donné rudement dans le cu. Autrefois, un *Tancrede*, un *Issé*, une *Europe galante*, les *Indes* et *Castor*, les *Talents Lyriques*, alloient a quatre, cinq, six mois. On ne voyait point la fin des representations d'une *Armide*. A present, tout cela vous tombe les uns sur les autres, comme des capucins de cartes. Aussi Rebel et Francœur jettent ils feu et flamme. Ils disent que tout est perdu, qu'ils sont ruinés; et que si l'on tolère plus longtems cette canaille chantante

de la foire, la musique nationale est au diable; et que l'Academie Royale du cul de sac n'a qu'a fermer boutique. Il y a bien quelque chose de vrai, la dedans. Les vieilles perruques qui viennent la depuis trente a quarante ans, tous les vendredis, au lieu de s'amuser comme ils ont fait par le passé, s'ennuyent et baillent sans trop scavoir pourquoi.[9]

∞   ∞   ∞

Philosophical dialogue, the essence of Enlightenment satire (of the Enlightenment in general) reveals one area where Socratic irony enjoys special favor. Hegel's study of *Le Neveu de Rameau* in the *Phenomenology of the Spirit* is a necessary starting point for an analysis of this theme. His inclusion of Diderot's satire in the chapter on *Aufklärung* as a key modern writing constitutes the invention of Diderot's work. It is required reading in any interpretation of Diderot. As Lukács has written: "...Hegel seized upon this work and was in fact one of the first to recognize its literary, intellectual and social merits. It cannot be by mere chance that Diderot's dialogue is the only modern work to be quoted in the *Phenomenology*."[10]

At the center of Hegel's reading are, of course, Lui and Moi. Their encounter is not the deaf and dumb theater of Enlightenment satire but a more fluid and problematical meeting typical of the middle and later part of the century. The subject raised in this encounter is self-consciousness, portrayed as it necessarily is on a mode of crisis. Moi plays a key role in this drama of self. He is to be taken, Hegel avers, as the "stable self": the one set in opposition to Lui.[11] Moi enjoys the self-assurance of those born to privilege and who see no difference between the destiny of the country they live in—the France of the eighteenth century—and world history. He accepts the permanent status of French culture and the timeless values of ethics and culture it embodies. Here are truths which give meaning to present reality and the future: that time when, after a few adjustments necessary to taste have been made, French values will be passed on intact to later generations (a point of view satirized by the narrator in the education scene with Lui, here, too, reminiscent of many passages in Rousseau). If

Moi is called "the happy self" it is not because he seeks pleasure. Happiness means stability, self-control, recognition of the need to subordinate the individual to the community.

Lui, by contrast, embodies the "unhappy consciousness" (*la conscience malheureuse* in Hippolyte's famous translation).[12] Lui's misfortune stems from his social condition, to be sure, and the curse of *la maudite molécule paternelle*. Yet it also has another source. The source is music. Music reveals the hold of an absolute more compelling than the pieties of French culture.

Rameau recognizes the power of these new areas. He can merge with them during moments like the *homme orchestre* scene. Yet Lui cannot grant them permanent aesthetic form (or understanding). His art is at best an intuitive one, based on the shadowy and brief mode of mime. Mime gives him a higher knowledge than his fellows, to be sure. But it also cuts him off from them, encouraging ostracism and self-hatred. Rameau is not, like Moi, a whole person or *citoyen*. His condition is at best that of *une âme déchirée:* one subject to an alienation of the mind (*une aliénation d'esprit*).[13]

The encounter between Lui and Moi sets into play a subjective idiom far more densely conceived than Marianne's strategies of *coquetterie* in Marivaux's novel of the same name or the different *examens de conscience* in *Les Liaisons dangereuses*. Through it, Diderot's story achieves a degree of self-awareness for which no previous eighteenth-century story could provide an example. It is an understanding of the contradictions of the historical moment in which Lui and Moi lived. The period is the Enlightenment.

Diderot's portrait of *Aufklärung* is not without its weaknesses or omissions, to be sure. As Lukács, one of the more consistently suggestive readers of Hegel has written, Diderot's account suffers from what is too great a degree of fluidity and movement. His story lacks dialectical control:

> the opposites [of *Rameau's Nephew*] continuously break down and merge with each other, thus exposing the nullity of all metaphysical notions about the solidity and permanence of the object world, the abstract identity of subjects with themselves, and reveal a continuous process of inversion with no direction best compared to a *perpetuum mobile*.[14]

Yet these, and doubtless other philosophical limitations, do not invalidate the force of Diderot's philosophical scheme, nor the originality of his conception. What Diderot has achieved in the few pages of dialogue between Lui and Moi is a full-scale portrait of the historical momentum of his own time and its special drama. It is the discovery of an instant of the decline of authority and the classical, and a shift into new modes of subjectivity and the modern.

As the Socratic features of Diderot's story strip away the bantering of early eighteenth-century satire, so too do they change the manner in which philosophical stories are narrated—what one can call the discourse of *philosophe* satire.

Traditional *philosophe* satire is a kind of intellectual theater. Subjects discussed are, like the theodicy or relativism, abstract. Characterization is wooden, based on characters who bear names like Candide or Martin meant to convey a philosophical position or point of view. The dialogue in which such characters are presented, though incomparably witty, is static. The reader knows at the outset that a given conversation will turn into an exchange of theses or position papers and that all exchanges will lead to a *dialogue des sourds*. Here lies a major priority of *philosophe* satire.

Diderot's comic style is far more self-critical and lively. It revolves, in fact, around a kind of critical farce. However outrageous or incomprehensible the outer appearance of a given passage (or encounter between Lui and Moi), there is always a measure of cohesiveness and depth.

Dialogue, for example, records the shock of an encounter whose meaning has yet to be fully mastered or understood. It emphasizes the ebb and flow of spoken discourse and a temporal scheme which is not the historical past but the more problematical (and valid) one of the present indicative.

Characterization undergoes change as well. Moi's naive but well-informed understanding of literary matters—though not of course musical ones—gives him a complexity usually denied straight-men in Diderot's other philosophical fictions (Jacques's master, for example, in *Jacques le fataliste*).[15] Lui's contortions of being make him into a novelistic figure. As Trilling has written, one is to take him as an early version of Dostoevsky's "underground man."[16]

Language is also revised. It expands from the restraints of classical satire to embrace the more demanding interests of the Socratic. The vocabulary of *Rameau's Nephew*, for example, is enormous. It uses words drawn from Italian opera and Latin (some of which like *O stercus pretiosum* and *Ingenii largitor venter* have a distinctly parodistic quality to them). Neologisms abound, as do examples of Parisian slang and terms taken from Diderot's native province of Burgundy. One finds too words of a scientific nature like *borborygme* and *composé* and many ironic proverbs like "Bonne renommée vaut mieux que ceinture dorée." And of course in references like "Dorat une fois après Freron, Palissot une fois après moi, Dorat vous deveniez stationnaire à côté de moi, pauvre plat bougre comme vous qui *siedo come un maestoso cazzo fra duoi coglioni,* " Diderot's text contains a solid dose of profanity as well.[17]

The most far-reaching change brought about by Socratic irony bears on the modernizing of *philosophe* satire which is the project of *Satyre 2de*. Here too opera enjoys pride of place. Its presence sparks one of those literary round-ups which the formalists have called a "carnival."[18] The many different comic influences and forms used by Diderot from Horace, La Bruyère, Voltaire, *le théâtre de la foire,* and Italian opera undergo stress, establish competing interests: interact. Soon a process of cross-fertilization or *hybridisation* gets under way:

> le mélange des styles...a quelque chose d'un accouplement entre espèces différentes...Tout se passe, dans l'univers *productif* de Diderot, comme si tous les éléments pouvaient non seulement s'attirer et se mêler, mais encore donner naissance à des êtres nouveaux.[19]

The result of this process is the creation of one of those *chèvre-pied* or "goat-footed" forms Diderot spoke of in *Le Rêve de d'Alembert*. The term builds on two meanings of satire (the goat-footed form par excellence). One is mythical and poetic, the other scientific and contemporary. Above all, the term draws attention to a key Socratic interest. It is the existence of a literary form impervious to genre.

∞ ∞ ∞

The novel for example, is surely unsatisfactory as a description of *Le Neveu de Rameau,* though some, like Daniel Mornet, have insisted on making use of it.[20] Diderot's story contains many techniques of a "novelistic" kind.[21] Among them are plural narrative voices, realistic psychology, and a probing into the uncertain origins of the story. Yet it lacks one feature which would turn the story into a novel. This feature is temporal complexity: the extension of narrative over a long period of time through which full psychological development and maturing of a character can occur.

The tale of Lui and Moi takes place only during a few moments or so. Its reference is to the period of time called *un après-dîner.* The kinship of Diderot's satire is more closely bound up with the "novelistic satires" which provide so lively a feature of eighteenth-century writing. Among them are *Les Lettres Persanes* (a work influenced by the epistolary novel) and *Candide.* The latter work contains a good deal of parody of novels. It is also portrayed as a "second" translation into French of an original story written in German by a certain Dr. Ralph, and thus endowed with a good helping of narrative irony.

Facétie is equally open to challenge. The term, as stated earlier, was used by Lanson as an all-purpose description of *philosophe* satire, an art which, he said, emphasized allegories and the kind of didactic fictions which were meant to "présenter aux gens du monde une idée abstraite ou un ensemble d'idées."[22] Yet *facétie* has many shortcomings of its own. The word is quite loose. *Facétie* can be used interchangeably with other labels meant to describe short comical tales like *opuscule* or *bleuette.* Moreover, the view of satire *facétie* conveys is a slight one—satire as a literary trifle, or weekend diversion. It is at odds with the more demanding and imaginatively probing vision of comedy one knows to have guided Diderot's literary interests.

Menippean satire would seem (at first glance at least) a more promising term. It was given prominence in North American countries in Frye's *The Anatomy of Criticism* (the chapter where he relates satire to a "theory of genres"). The menippean has also been used as a central reference by Bakhtin (*Rabelais and His World*) and Kristeva.[23]

Frye's definition of menippean satire is especially clear:

> The Menippean deals less with people as such than with mental attitudes. Pedants, bigots, cranks, parvenus, virtuosi, enthusiasts, rapacious and incompetent professional men of all kinds, are handled in terms of their occupational approach to life as distinct from their social behavior.
>
> Petronius, Apuleius, Rabelais, Swift, and Voltaire all use a loose-jointed narrative form often confused with the romance. It differs from the romance, however...as it is not primarily concerned with the exploits of heroes, but relies on the free play of intellectual fancy and the kind of humorous observation that produces caricature. It differs also from the picaresque form, which has the novel's interest in the actual structure of society. At its most concentrated, the Menippean satire presents us with a vision of the world in terms of a single intellectual pattern. The intellectual structure built up from the story makes for violent dislocations in the customary logic of narrative, though the appearance of carelessness that results reflects only the carelessness of the reader or his tendency to judge by a novel-centered conception of fiction.[24]

Yet here too major problems of validity arise. The scope of the menippean is one of them. As defined by those who use the term, the menippean embraces short fictional tales drawn from so many periods and styles as to make it impossibly eclectic. Frye, for example, lists *Candide, The Way of All Flesh, Gulliver's Travels, Point Counterpoint, Brave New World,* and *The Satyricon* as examples of the genre (in addition of course to Burton's *The Anatomy of Melancholy).* Bakhtin fills out the list with Dostoevsky and Rabelais. Kristeva's references are equally generous. She includes in the menippean several texts drawn from a "modern" satirical canon. Among them are *Ulysses, The Castle,* and Bataille's short novels.

Other difficulties can be mentioned as well. Carnival writing or *carnavalisation* is often substituted for menippean satire in discussions of specific literary texts. "Polyphonic novel" and the menippean are not infrequently taken to be synonymous, thus blurring distinctions between works which are indeed novels (however ambiguous such a term might be) and those which are only "novelistic."[25] Even more disturbing, however, is a reliance on classification which seems to border on a quest for a literary absolute. However exotic or uneven any literary text is, it can be dissected through the menippean and ultimately brought into line.

That such a scheme has great value cannot be denied. Use of the menippean allows readers to distinguish between "controlled fictions" (as Scholes has called them) and stories of a more freely imaginative kind.[26] The reference to the menippean helps one understand an unusual paradox in French literary history. It is the way writings of an unclassifiable or transgressive nature are made part of a second pantheon of radical texts. The latter canon stands alongside traditional masterpieces as a "darker" tradition. It thus allows French literature to be integrated into a single and continuous whole, to be passed on from one generation to the next.[27]

But use of the term menippean cannot but hinder, if not indeed falsify, readings of works which resist integration into such pantheons. Works of this kind are conceived as having properties which place them outside even so broad a label as the menippean. *Rameau's Nephew* is one such text. Diderot's story is not merely another example of an erratic comic tale. The work contains markings of a uniquely Socratic nature. They push satire to what is indeed a goat-footed form. It is a story *beyond genre*.

Beyond genre does not of course mean a work whose inner contradictions (or longings) transcend literary form. Such a view of literary creation would be a romantic one, suggestive of a split between subject matter and literary representation (literature and being). It has already been undercut in the various doubles and plays of irony to which the *homme orchestre* scene gave rise.

What beyond genre suggests is a more limited, though by no means less critically acute, state. It is a work of literature which *refuses* genre. For genre, in the case of *Le Neveu de Rameau,* French *philosophe* satire, and the Latin tradition on which it is modeled, offers only a shallow version of comical writing: one shaped by neoclassical expectations about the value of comedy as a literary genre and of irony as a rhetorical mode.

The narrator of Diderot's story, however, comes to realize how constricted this view is, how it stifles the powers of comic invention of which satire and irony are capable. These powers are achieved when satire frees itself from reliance on the past and functions in an independent way.

Two examples of a satiric form unbidden to genre may be found in fact in *Le Neveu de Rameau.* Italian opera is one of them. The art is unorthodox in the extreme, and radically un-French. Socratic philosophizing is another. The mode is devoted to unwritten philosophical tracts and a use of questions which cast doubt on the very possibility of philosophy.

The one satiric form is Italian, the other Greek. Music provides the sustaining interest of the first; philosophy of the second. Both approaches come together through a common validation of irony and the comic. The meeting is the authentic synthesis sought in so many parts of Diderot's story and not the bogus *réunion des arts* put on, and as quickly rejected, in the one-man show. The result of this fusion of music and philosophy—the ancient and the modern—is *Satyre 2de:* second or Socratic satire.

∞ ∞ ∞

One feature of Second *Satyre* enjoys special significance. It is brevity. For all the complexity of narrative idiom revealed in the work, the rich suggestiveness of its philosophical framework, Diderot's tale is extremely short. The Fabre edition, a masterful work of research, contains at best one hundred pages of text. An acting version of *Rameau* takes a few hours to stage. When set alongside the other fictions with which Diderot's story is inevitably, and correctly, compared—*La Religieuse, Jacques le fataliste, Les Bijoux Indiscrets*—the work seems slight indeed.

In brevity, of course, lies a favored form of Socratic irony: the emptying out of the expectations and traditions of a known literary genre. The genre is philosophical satire. Henceforth slightness of form will not be proof that a given work is a *facétie*. Brevity will now be the sign of extreme compression, compactness: proof indeed of a strategy of *rétrécissement et expansion*.[28]

Packed into the few pages of dialogue between Lui and Moi, inserted into a tale whose outer appearance is that of an inconsequential outing among the chess players of the Palais Royal in the heyday of Louis Quinze, is a story no less complete or rigorous because of the frailty of its structure or the extravagance of its comic effects. The story is the tale of satire.

The narrator's insights into *Aufklärung* are part of this "satire of satires," to be sure. They take philosophical narrative away from inquiries into why Lisbon was levelled in the middle of the eighteenth century or why Tahitians do not think like priests, into an appraisal of history and self-consciousness. References to "Diderot" give the work an autobiographical, even confessional, tone required in many writings of the later part of the century from Rousseau and Laclos to Diderot's own fictions like *Le Rêve de d'Alembert* (where Diderot is, of course, a central character) and the meditation on Seneca called *L'Essai sur les règnes de Claude et de Néron*.

The survey of satire as a form is no less a part of this Socratic text. It is structured as a carnival. And the different forms the narrator collects (and parodies) make *Le Neveu de Rameau* into a kind of encyclopedia of satirical techniques as well as a textbook to Enlightenment comic theater and mime.

Dialogue gives these concerns momentum and pacing. The present tense inevitably used in the work confers upon them a mood of crisis. Borrowings from mime and opera add color (and a sense of the unexpected). Diderot's story even comes into possession of a kind of poetics foreign to *philosophe* satire.

Nor is this poetic side the result of musical prose or the fury of *l'homme orchestre* scene alone. Poetic satire derives from the Socratic interests of Diderot's story. For it is a mode which is inseparable from prophecy and visionary lyricism. It gives to Diderot's little story the feel of a work about to shift from the old structures of Horace and neoclassical tragedy into new arrangements (and forms) of an *enharmonic* kind.[29] "Premières lueurs" best conveys this mood.[30] The words, not surprisingly perhaps, are spoken by Lui. They signify first glimmerings of beliefs and forms as yet unworked into final control and understanding.

Yet these glimmerings are not will o' the wisps or deceptions. They point to the reality of a work centered on key changes of history and consciousness. They also reveal the presence of a unique literary structure toward which *Le Neveu de Rameau* has been moving through its many different *dédoublements* and ironic turns. It is a kind of Socratic or comic opera whose "libretto" is the story of comic irony and the discovery of the new.

An observation by George Steiner seems to sum up the point of this Socratic satire, and the connections between music and irony on which it is based, with special insight. It comes from a book called, with an appropriately operatic title, *Bluebeard's Castle:*

> Conceivably, an ancient circle is closing. In his *Mythologiques,* Lévi-Strauss has asserted that melody holds the key to the "mystère suprême de l'homme." Grasp the riddle of melodic invention, of our apparently imprinted sense of harmonic accord, and you will touch on the roots of human consciousness. Only music, says Lévi-Strauss, is a primal universal language, at once comprehensible to all and untranslatable into any other idiom. Speech comes later than music; even before the disorder at Babel, it was part of the Fall of man. This supposition is, itself, immemorial. It is fundamental to Orphic and Pythagorean doctrines, to the *harmonia mundi* of Boethius and the sixteenth century. It guided Kepler and was inferred almost as a commonplace in Condillac's great *Essai sur l'Origine des Connaissances Humaines* of 1746. It is no accident that the two visionaries most observant of the crises of the classic order, Kierkegaard and Nietzsche, should have seen in music the mode of pre-eminent energy and meaning.[31]

VI

Conclusion

From Satire to Irony

WITH THE WRITING OF *LE NEVEU DE RAMEAU*, a permanent change comes over French comic fiction of the eighteenth century which parallels and completes the upheaval in musical circles brought about with the arrival of the *buffoni*. The change is the metamorphosis of satire.

This form, the embodiment of *philosophe* interests in comedy, polemical storytelling and, in works like *Candide* and *Les Lettres Persanes,* the symbol of the Enlightenment's achievement in literature, is overthrown from its position as a slight genre given to dead-end conversations, burlesque adventures, and a view of comic irony as bantering wit.

As revised by Diderot's second version of the form, satire maps out interests of an aesthetic as well as philosophical kind. The affinities the form displays are with the novel rather than Horatian satire (or Voltaire). Indeed, with *Le Neveu de Rameau,* satire falls away from its position as a mere genre or, another favored way of describing it, a "vehicle for local wit, a means of adding brilliance to discourse or of making a point."[1] Satire is now an independent *Socratic mode*.[2]

Socratic satire brings to literature many complex strategies of self-conscious narration and "deconstruction." It favors the creation of an original, and seemingly unclassifiable, literary form of an operatic kind. Above all, Socratic writing changes the face of comic irony: the backbone of satire and the vision of art it seeks to convey.

Irony has now broken away from the contrasts between manichean and deist ("micro" and "mega") set out by *philosophes* with almost automatic regularity as a means of illustrating the dual or split nature of comedy. The influence of opera and the Socratic has caused irony to modulate into a new key of integration and dialectics.

Irony draws on sources rooted in history rather than exoticism or fantasy. Its masks and *dédoublements,* though extravagant and hard to disentangle, are inseparable from an enterprise of self-exploration[3] and, in conversations like that of Lui and Moi, a measure of self-understanding as well. Indeed the ties irony establishes with music and passion relate it to a search for transcendence and, in scenes like *l'homme orchestre,* a poetic absolute.

Friedrich Schlegel, one of Diderot's most sympathetic, and, it would appear, overlooked, readers, recognized the originality of these interests and the view of irony they were meant to endorse. His *Letter on Poetry* contains the following appraisal of *Jacques le fataliste,* a work whose Sternian overtones made it an especially attractive vehicle for discussion of irony and comic transcendence. The work contains, Schlegel wrote,

> a store-house of *Witz* uncontaminated by mere sentiment. Diderot's story is told with keen intelligence and taken in hand by the surest of touches. It is, I would say without exaggeration, a work of art. By art I do not mean sublime poetry but arabesque. Yet this is precisely why, in my view, Diderot's story is so important. For I hold arabesque to be fundamental to poetry....[4]

Schlegel's comments are not without a controversial side, to be sure. His use of terms like *Witz*[5] and arabesque is often unclear. Schlegel mixes references to the poetic and the prosaic in perhaps too summary a manner. He does not even mention *Le Neveu de Rameau* by name (nor can one be certain whether he read it). Yet his reading is no less vital to an understanding of Diderot's text. For it draws attention to a development in European aesthetics which took place in the middle and declining years of the eighteenth century and in which *Le Neveu de Rameau* played an exemplary role. The development is the emptying out of *philosophe* irony, the irony of the Enlightenment as one ought to call it, and its replacement by a more Socratic and poetic version known as "romantic irony." Lilian Furst describes the change with special insight:

It was only at the turn of the eighteenth century that irony suddenly assumed a prominent position. It lagged forty or more years behind such concepts as "genius," originality," and "creativity" which had sprung into the limelight soon after the middle of the century in a cluster of aesthetic treatises from which irony was conspicuously absent. The Age of Sensibility doubtless preferred the warmth of a tender heart to the coolness of an ironic mind. When irony burst onto the intellectual scene, it was in a different place and an altered format: from the lowly primers of rhetoric it moved to the lofty tomes of speculative aesthetics, and its model switched from the Latin to the Greek, from Cicero and Quintilian to Socrates and Plato. The year 1797, with the publication of Friedrich Schlegel's *Lyceum* fragments, has been cited as the turning-point in the European history of the concept of irony. Schlegel's *Lyceum* collection, together with his *Athenäum* fragments (1798) and his *Ideen* (1800), accomplished a metamorphosis of irony by presenting it in a new context and with new functions.[6]

The full story of *Le Neveu de Rameau* is thus the tale of the birth of irony as much as it is a chapter in the history of French opera, a report on the rise of self-consciousness or a study of *ressentiment* and social parasitism.[7]

With the uncovering of this second interest, Diderot's narrative returns to the starting point illustrated in the original quotation from Horace: "Vertumnis, quotquot sunt, natus iniquis." At issue here is an exemplary story, one that sums up and provides an ideal form for a given literary tradition.

Diderot's story rejects of course the Horatian or Voltairian model. Here are false ancestors already displaced through the ironic turns of Diderot's story—in the case of Horace, in fact, used as an instance of a once powerful classical source reduced to a scrap of learning cited with the disdain reserved for some of the choicer passages of French opera in the *homme orchestre* scene.

The example Diderot's story holds to is the more problematical one validated by its Socratic ancestry. The example invites consideration of Italian music and opera, to be sure. It also suggests the importance of a key companion to Socratic writing whose exploitation is never far from any corner of the story. This companion is modernity.

Like satire, the term modernity has dual properties that make it difficult to anatomize or define. On the one hand, modernity invokes a specific literary period or movement. It is the one sketched out in Baudelaire's *flâneurs,* dandies and other "heroes in decay," Flaubert's stories of banality and nothingness, and Proust's researches into past time. Here was developed, as Connolly has said, "a spirit which combined certain intellectual qualities inherited from the Enlightenment: lucidity, irony, scepticism, intellectual curiosity, combined with the passionate intensity and enhanced sensibility of the Romantics, their rebellion and sense of technical experiment, their awareness of living in a tragic age."[8]

On the other hand, modernity transcends literary handbooks. An interest in the new is by no means a recent one. Recognition of the power of change informs virtually all of the great texts in the French canon, from Montaigne's meditation on the meaning of America ("Des Cannibales"), the passionate inquiries of La Bruyère into the lives of peasants, and Descartes' philosophy of criticism and the self. In many ways, as Ernest Curtius has suggested in *European Literature and the Latin Middle Ages,* modernity is not a contemporary reference at all. It is a universal topos.[9]

Yet there can surely be little question as to the central claim of modernity, nor the affinities it establishes with Diderot's story. Modernity is not only congenial to the satiric and the Socratic. It is *inseparable* from it.

Works conceived in a modern vein validate low or fallen genres like the novel. The characters whose lives are detailed in such tales are problematical outsiders whose status is in flux. Modern works emphasize a rhetoric of irony and dissonance, and a vision that has been pried loose from classical necessity and essence. Above all, modern writings map out an ancestry, or way of relating to the past, which denies the comfortable "filial" pattern of a *Querelle des Anciens et des Modernes:* two hostile views of aesthetics and existence set against each other in a mock battle requiring an allegiance and choice.[10]

The ancestry staked out by *Le Neveu de Rameau* is of a more oblique kind. The term "nephew" best sums it up. The reference allows Diderot to dramatize the special "anxiety" characteristic of modern works, to be sure.[11] It speaks to an originality which invests "its trust in the power of the present moment as an origin, but discovers that, in severing itself from the past, it has at the same time severed itself from the present."[12] Above all, though, when set in the full carnival structure of *Le Neveu de Rameau,* the nephew allusion achieves an even deeper meaning. Its presence conveys a full genealogy of the modern movement. And it is all the more vital and imaginatively probing because of the way in which this history is structured. It is as a kind of Socratic opera with a distinct poetic and visionary bias. The work's alliances are no longer with Voltaire or Horace at all. They are with key documents of music and the coming of the new. Among them are *The Birth of Tragedy* and *Either/Or.*

A story as rich in Socratic ironies as *Le Neveu de Rameau* will not lend itself to final conclusions, definitive framing statements, or other *discours de clôture* always satirized in Diderot from the feeble rebuttals of Moi to the *redites* and maunderings of Jacques's master in *Jacques le fataliste.*

Readings that remain faithful to the pluralities of the Socratic—a mode which is not one of infinite deconstruction or "incommensurability"[13] but of obedience to the more limited gains of dialectics—seem appropriate when, as is necessary in a literary essay, a stopping point has been reached.

A reading of this kind can be found in a work not usually thought of as related to the French eighteenth century (much less Diderot). The work is Walter Benjamin's study of German Baroque drama called *The Origin of German Tragic Drama.* The text was written in the early 1920s and has come to be thought of as a central meditation on modernity. "It is, moreover, precisely the more significant works," wrote Benjamin, "in as much as they are not the original and so to speak ideal embodiments of the genre which fall outside the limits of genre. A major work will either establish the genre or abolish it, and the perfect work will do both."[14]

The notion of a major literary work outside its own genre is an intriguing aspect of Benjamin's statement, to be sure. Equally thought-provoking are his comments about the irregularity which characterizes many works in the modern canon. The more suggestive formulation though, is surely Benjamin's use of the work "perfect." Perfect implies no formal balance or ethical purpose. It suggests a more ironic and paradoxical state. The condition is that of a work of art which both invents its genre and brings it to an end.

Yet as Diderot has a character observe in *Jacques le fataliste,* "un paradoxe n'est pas toujours une fausseté."[15] *Le Neveu de Rameau* does indeed achieve this dual, and only apparently contradictory, state. Diderot's story finishes off satire as an Enlightenment or Voltairian genre. It creates it anew as an ironic mode where philosophy and music, *les anciens et les modernes,* come together through the unique influence of Socrates (and opera) and in which can be seen the first stirrings of romantic interests to dominate the century to come.

Socratic and perfect, then. Here are the last of the many doubles which sustain the tale of Lui and Moi. With their appearance, the wiles of Vertumnis, the god of chance and, as now seems clear, of irony as well, are played out. Satire, the single exemplary form of *philosophe* literature, has been abolished and reinvented. One can now read *Le Neveu de Rameau* as it was intended to be. The text is Diderot's finest literary work, a satire of satires, and the "perfect" or exemplary comic writing of the French eighteenth century.

Notes

Chapter I: Diderot and Satire

1. The bibliography on satire, as one might expect, is enormous. A useful survey of studies on the subject, one covering the period from 1900 to 1971, may be found in Ingrid Hantsch, "Bibliographie zur Gattungspoetik (2): Theorie des Satire (1900-1971)," *Zeitschrift für Französische Sprache und Literatur,* LXXXII (1972), pp. 153-56. Three critical writings are of exceptional interest to an analysis of satire as a literary genre. They are Northrop Frye's *Anatomy of Criticism* (Princeton: Princeton Univ. Press, 1957); M. Bakhtin's *Rabelais and His World* (Cambridge: MIT, 1968); and Julia Kristeva's *Semeiotike* (Paris: Seuil, 1969).

2. The phrase "littérature et philosophie" comes from Jean Starobinski's landmark article on Diderot, "Le Philosophe, le géomètre, l'hybride," *Poétique,* XXI (1975), pp. 8-23.

3. For Voltaire and the *facétie* see Diana Guiragossian, *Voltaire's Facéties* (Geneva: Droz, 1963).

4. The historical background of the Diderot-Socrates relationship is discussed by Raymond Trousson, *Socrate devant Voltaire, Diderot et Rousseau: La Conscience en face du mythe* (Paris: Minard, 1967). Cf. Stephen Werner, "Diderot: Les Derniers Ecrits" in *Diderot: Les Dernières Œuvres,* ed. Peter France and Anthony Strugnell (Edinburgh: Edinburgh Univ. Press, 1985), pp. 171-79.

5. For the "invention" of modernity see W. Jackson Bate, *The Burden of the Past and the English Poet* (New York: Norton, 1970).

6. Diderot uses the term in *Le Rêve de d'Alembert* as an example of a poetic hybrid. *Chèvre-pied* also underscores an interest in breaking out of genres validated throughout the *œuvre*.

7. *Candide,* probably the most famous comic writing of the eighteenth century, is one such problematical text. Virtually all of the labels used to describe short fictional tales of a didactic kind from "menippean satire" to *le conte philosophique* (even the novel) have been applied to it. The specific genre affiliation of Voltaire's masterpiece is still open to discussion (though "menippean satire" probably best defines its literary surface). *Les Lettres Persanes* is another elusive text. The work is both an epistolary novel, related to themes articulated in *La Princesse de Clèves* and a sociological inquiry or pamphlet containing discussions of colonialism and dueling. *Les Rêveries du promeneur solitaire* is similarly ambiguous. This story is at once a missing chapter from *Les Confessions* and an example of a new genre of *prose lyrique.*

8. For the background of the *roman galant* see Marie-Louise Dufrenoy, *L'Orient romanesque en France, 1704-1789* (Montréal: Editions Beauchemin, 1946-47), pp. 107-20. Important observations can be found too in Robert J. Ellrich, "The Structure of Diderot's *Les Bijoux indiscrets,*" *Romanic Review,* 52 (1961), pp. 279-89, and the critical edition of the novel edited by Aram Vartanian in the Hermann series.

9. The central study of this second story, impounded in the main text, is still Herbert Dieckmann's "The Préface-Annexe of *La Religieuse,*" *Diderot Studies,* II (1953), pp. 21-147.

10. Two recent studies have attempted to explore the meaning of this anti-novel. For the concept of mimesis and representation see Thomas Kavanagh, "The Vacant Mirror: A Study of Mimesis through Diderot's *Jacques le fataliste,*" *Studies on Voltaire,* 104 (1973). Stephen Werner's "Diderot's 'Great Scroll': Narrative Art in *Jacques le fataliste,*" *Studies on*

Voltaire, 128 (1975) looks into the issue of the *grand rouleau* and the notion of a "novel of novels."

11. Herbert Dieckmann's critical edition of the *Supplément* (Geneva: Droz, 1955) has many stimulating comments about the genesis of the *conte philosophique.*

12. A key study of this work, one of Diderot's earliest philosophical contributions, and a text of much importance for the development of his mature ideas, is the critical edition of Robert Niklaus (Geneva: Droz, 1951). See also D. J. Adams, *Diderot, Dialogue and Debate* (Liverpool: Francis Cairns, 1986).

13. Two studies of *Le Rêve* are essential. They are the critical edition of Paul Vernière (Paris: M. Didier, 1951); and the long essay of Herbert Dieckmann, *Die Kunstlerische Form des Rêve de d'Alembert* (Köln: Westdeutscher Verlag, 1966). The general relationship of Diderot to Lucretius is explored in C. A. Fusil, "Lucrèce et les philosophes du XVIIIe siècle," *Revue de l'histoire littéraire,* 35 (1928), pp. 194-210; and Gustav R. Hocke, *Lukrez in Frankreich von der Renaissance bis zur Revolution* (Köln: Buchdruckerei Dr. Paul Kerschgens, 1935), pp. 151-53.

14. The most suggestive account of this work is the article of Werner Krauss, "Zu einer Prosa Diderots," *Sinn und Form,* 14 (1962), pp. 161-86.

15. An excellent introduction to this work is the essay of J. Robert Loy, "L'Essai sur les règnes de Claude et de Néron," *Cahiers de l'association internationale des études françaises,* 13 (1961), pp. 239-54.

16. These aspects are developed by Stephen Werner in "Irony and the Essay: Diderot's 'Essai sur ma vieille robe de chambre,' " in *Diderot: Digression and Dispersion,* ed. Jack Undank and Herbert Josephs (Lexington: French Forum, 1984), pp. 269-77.

17. Lionel Trilling, *Sincerity and Authenticity* (Cambridge: Harvard Univ. Press, 1972), p. 27.

18. Denis Diderot, *Le Neveu de Rameau,* ed. Jean Fabre (Geneva: Droz, 1963), p. 3. As the Hermann series has yet to publish a critical edition of *Rameau's Nephew,* Fabre's text will be the one used in this essay. All references to Diderot's satire come from Fabre's edition. Also of unquestioned value to students of Diderot's satire is the edition of *Le Neveu de Rameau* by Jacques Chouillet (Paris: Imprimerie Nationale, 1981).

19. Northrop Frye, "The Nature of Satire," *University of Toronto Quarterly,* XIV (Oct. 1944), p. 75.

20. A neat summary of this view of Diderot may be found in Otis Fellows, *Diderot* (New York: Twayne, 1977), pp. 17-19.

21. Roger Zuber, "La Satire," *Encyclopaedia Universalis,* Paris, 1968, XIV, p. 691.

22. Gustave Lanson, *L'Art de la prose* (Paris: Arthème Fayard, 1907), p. 176.

23. Donal O'Gorman, *Diderot the Satirist* (Toronto: Univ. of Toronto Press, 1971), pp. 3-17.

24. Michael Riffaterre, *Le Style des Pléiades de Gobineau* (New York: Columbia Univ. Press, 1957). See especially, pp. 75-77. "L'archaïsme a ceci de particulier que son expressivité ou son caractère esthétique vient du fait que son réemploi momentané n'atténue pas son aspect obsolète: ni l'écrivain ni son lecteur ne cessent d'y voir un vocable vieilli."

25. An annotated bibliography of articles and books on *Le Neveu de Rameau* written in the period from 1950 to 1983 may be found in the

excellent study of D. J. Adams, "*Le Neveu de Rameau* since 1950," *Studies on Voltaire and the Eighteenth Century,* 217 (1983) pp. 371-87.

Chapter II: Horatian Satire

1. The best study of Horace and Diderot is the essay appended to Ernst Curtius's *European Literature and the Latin Middle Ages* (New York: Pantheon, 1953), pp. 573-83. A more general study of Horace's influence on *Rameau's Nephew* is that of Karl Maurer in "Die Satire in der Weise des Horaz als Kunstform von Diderots *Neveu de Rameau,*" *Romanische Forschungen,* LXIV (1952), pp. 365-404. For epigraphs in Diderot see Jane Marsh Dieckmann, " 'A Zerbina penserete': A note on Diderot's epigraph," in *Studies in Eighteenth-Century French Literature presented to Robert Niklaus,* ed. J. H. Fox, M. H. Waddicor, and D. A. Watts (Exeter: Univ. of Exeter, 1975), pp. 43-47.

2. Horace, *Satires, Epistles and Ars Poetica* (Cambridge: Harvard Univ. Press, 1957), p. 470. The translation of these lines is as follows: "Such is the power of order and connection, such the beauty that may crown the common-place."

3. *Ibid.,* p. 24. The quotation comes from the *Satires,* I:2.

4. Diderot, *Le Neveu de Rameau,* p. 3.

5. Joseph Riddel develops a suggestive reading of the *en-têtes* and their relationship to the larger text in an essay entitled "Pound and the Decentered Image," *The Georgia Review,* XXIX (Fall, 1975), p. 565.

6. Jean Marmier, *Horace en France au XVIIe siècle* (Paris: PUF, 1962), pp. 267-300.

7. For a general introduction to Roman satire see *Satire: Critical Essays on Roman Literature,* ed. J. P. Sullivan (Bloomington: Indiana Univ. Press, 1963), p. 1.

8. Sir James Frazer, *The Golden Bough* (New York: Anchor, 1957), p. 319.

9. Two studies of Rameau's "uncle" are essential to an understanding of Diderot's text. They are Cuthbert Girdlestone, *Jean-Philippe Rameau* (New York: Dover, 1969) and the recent monograph by Jean-Jacques Robrieux, "Jean-Philippe Rameau et l'opinion philosophique en France au dix-huitième siècle," *Studies on Voltaire and the Eighteenth Century,* 238 (1985), pp. 273-394.

10. Diderot, *Le Neveu de Rameau,* p. 4.

11. For genius in Diderot, see Herbert Dieckmann, "Diderot's Conception of Genius," *Journal of the History of Ideas,* 2 (1941), pp. 151-82; and Otis Fellows, "The Theme of Genius in Diderot's *Neveu de Rameau,*" *Diderot Studies,* II (1952), pp. 168-99.

12. Diderot, *Le Neveu de Rameau,* p. 11.

13. Roger Laufer, "Structure et signification du *Neveu de Rameau,*" *Revue des Sciences Humaines,* XXV (1960), pp. 399-413.

14. Diderot, *Le Neveu de Rameau,* p. 24.

15. *Ibid.,* p. 75.

16. *Ibid.,* pp. 51-52.

17. *Ibid.,* p. 76.

18. For the *querelle des bouffons* see Louisette Richebourg, *Contribution à l'histoire de la Querelle des Bouffons* (Paris: Nizet et Bastard, 1937); Servando Sacaluga, "Diderot, Rousseau et la querelle musicale de 1752," *Diderot Studies,* X (1968), pp. 133-73; and Georges Snyders, *Le goût musical en France au XVIIe et XVIIIe siècles* (Paris: Vrin, 1968).

19. Diderot, *Le Neveu de Rameau,* p. 81.

20. *Ibid.,* p. 79.

21. *Ibid.,* p. 88.

22. *Ibid.,* p. 107.

23. *Ibid.,* p. 109.

24. Jack Undank and Herbert Josephs, *Diderot: Digression and Dispersion* (Lexington: French Forum, 1984).

25. Diderot, *Le Neveu de Rameau,* p. 3.

26. *Ibid.,* p. 4.

27. The chessboard symbolizes this binary discourse (in addition, of course, to recalling Diderot's own interest in chess and his familiarity with Philidor, a famous chess player—and opera composer—mentioned in the text). The chessboard is closed-in and dual. The point of the *homme orchestre* passage is to dissolve this structure through the ironies of pantomime and music.

28. Littré defines a *période* in the following manner: "Terme de grammaire. Assemblage de propositions liées entre elles par des conjonctions, et qui toutes ensemble font un sens fini, dit aussi sens complet." One of the examples used to illustrate this definition comes from La Bruyère: "Le commun des hommes aime les phrases et les périodes."

29. Parataxis is not, of course, an invention of the eighteenth century. It provided a standard rhetorical feature of the late seventeenth century (as described by Lamy in *L'Art de parler,* ed. 1712, p. 152; and Rollin, *De la Manière d'enseigner et d'étudier les Belles Lettres,* ed. 1732, II, p. 220). The originality of Diderot's use of the form lies in the violence

he brings to it: the strangeness of a rhetorical device used to emphasize a kind of excess which cannot be integrated into classical language.

30. Fabre (p. 261) points out the scientific origins of this word and says that *composé* began to take on moral shadings only toward the end of the eighteenth century. "L'emploi de cet adjectif substantivé, longtemps confiné dans ses acceptions purement scientifiques, ne s'est étendu au vocabulaire moral que vers la fin du XVIIIe siècle."

31. The cliché status of the passage derives from the narrator's use of heroic or noble epithets in a low or realistic context. It gives the passage a mock-heroic tone crucial to parody.

32. *Après-dîner* lacks a clear temporal reference. Use of the indefinite pronoun "un" reinforces its vagueness. This is, of course, the central point of the passage. Diderot's text strives to convey a brooding and indeterminate mood, a period of a problematic kind, somewhere between noon and dusk.

33. La Bruyère is a central (and generally overlooked) influence on *Le Neveu de Rameau*. The connection comes through a common interest in portraits and comic *tableaux* as well as various stylistic affinities. The main one is the repetition of the pronoun "il" in the *homme orchestre* scene.

34. *Pensées* is an *effet de style*. It introduces an element of vagueness and free-floating association. As such, the term has an ironic effect. It provides a dramatic contrast with the more formal mode of *la pensée:* an area of understanding presumably outside comedy and satire.

35. Diderot, *Le Neveu de Rameau,* p. 3.

36. Intensification is related to the rhetorical device known as anaphora. The device is often used to create an ironic—and comic—effect.

37. Diderot, *Le Neveu de Rameau,* p. 16.

38. *Dédoublement* does not have an exact English translation, though "doubling" and "twinning" are close approximations. The term emphasizes the kind of splitting common to self-conscious narratives. *Dédoublement* also helps favor the creation of a fictional self-portrait.

39. Peter France, *Rhetoric and Truth in France: Descartes to Diderot* (Oxford: Clarendon, 1972), pp. 191-234.

40. Julia Kristeva, *Semeiotike* (Paris: Seuil, 1969), p. 158.

41. *Ibid.*

42. The story thus emphasizes the openness which characterizes so many novels of the time, from *Manon Lescaut* to *Les Liaisons dangereuses*. Diderot's story validates a problematical self rather than one able to engage in a "constitution du moi." It confirms an inability to overcome the past through the "truth of fiction" (what Girard has called, in a highly stimulating essay, an ironic play between *mensonge romantique* and *vérité romanesque*).

43. Classical plural is, of course, an oxymoron. For classical writings strive for clarity and truth. Yet the term does seem to provide a fitting image for the tone of the first pages of *Rameau* and the problematical contrasts between past and present, classical and "romantic" it introduces. Roland Barthes, *S/Z* (Paris: Seuil, 1970), p. 14.

44. Diderot, *Le Neveu de Rameau,* p. 82.

45. Herbert Josephs, *Diderot's Dialogue of Language and Gesture* (Columbus: Ohio State Univ. Press, 1969), p. 163.

Chapter III: *L'homme orchestre*

1. Diderot. *Le Neveu de Rameau,* pp. 82-83.

2. *Le théâtre de la foire* or Parisian fairground theater is a central influence on Diderot's story. The art lies behind many of the comic routines of Lui and the popular humor which sustains so much of the irony of *Le Neveu de Rameau*. A useful introduction to the subject (set against the background of comic opera) can be found in Martin Cooper, *Opéra Comique* (London: Max Parrish, 1949), ch. 1. The chapter is devoted to what Cooper calls "The Comedians of the Fair."

3. Diderot, *Le Neveu de Rameau*, pp. 20-21; p. 48.

4. Mime is closely connected to farce. It requires exaggerated caricature of social situations and social types. Descriptions of this kind run a full gamut from burlesque to the more outrageous comic fantasies of *l' homme orchestre* scene.

5. Diderot, *Le Neveu de Rameau*, p. 84.

6. *Ibid.*, p. 85. The passage foreshadows the interest in synaesthesia which will play so crucial a role in nineteenth-century aesthetics from Baudelaire to Huysmans. Synaesthesia stresses a wilful distortion of aesthetic categories. In the case of Diderot's example, it is a search for an impossible form, one which gives voice to that which is soundless.

7. D. J. Adams, *Diderot, Dialogue and Debate*, pp. 140-62.

8. Denis Diderot, *Œuvres complètes*, (Paris: Assézat-Tourneux, 1875-77), I, p. 357.

9. Jean-Jacques Rousseau, *Œuvres complètes* (Paris: Belin, 1793), vol. XIX, p. 49. Rousseau explicitly says in this work that theater is an illusion. It provides a false catharsis. Classical theater cures spectators, he avers, of passions they do not have. It encourages (*fomenter* is the word used by Rousseau) passions they do suffer from. Rousseau uses an example drawn from ancient history to illustrate this state. It is the Roman emperor who wept at an especially moving part of a play he had just

seen and, on the very evening after the performance, set about executing various political enemies with perfect calm.

10. Diderot, *Le Neveu de Rameau,* p. 4.

11. An excellent reading of the aesthetic (and political) problems raised by Rousseau's study can be found in Patrick Coleman, *Rousseau's Political Imagination: Rule and Representation in La Lettre à d'Alembert* (Geneva: Droz: 1984).

12. Jacques Chouillet's Diderot studies are essential for an understanding of this issue. See *La Formation des idées esthétiques de Diderot* (Paris: Colin, 1973) and *L'Esthétique des Lumières* (Paris: PUF, 1974).

13. Diderot, *Œuvres complètes,* (Assézat et Tourneux) III, 511-12.

14. Diderot, *Le Neveu de Rameau,* p. 84.

15. *Ibid.,* p. 265.

16. The fact that the scene is staged in a public place is surely not accidental. Public theater expands the classical *mise en scène* from the enclosed space of "administrative theater." It provides the more natural setting favored by ancient Greek theater, Renaissance city plays, and, of course, "le théâtre de la foire." An interest in theater of this kind can be found in writers of a far less "romantic" bent than Diderot. Burke is one of them. In his essay on the sublime he articulates a distinction between "conventional theater" and a "theater of nature."

17. Jean-Jacques Robrieux emphasizes connections between opera and politics in "Jean-Philippe Rameau et l'opinion philosophique en France au dix-huitième siècle," *Studies on Voltaire and the Eighteenth Century,* 238 (1985).

18. Rousseau, *Œuvres complètes,* p. 41. A fine study of this problem can be found in Jean Rousset, "Qu'est-ce que le talent du

comédien?" *Annales Jean-Jacques Rousseau,* 37 (1966-68), pp. 19-34. "Cette question," Rousset writes, "Rousseau la pose au centre de sa *Lettre sur les spectacles,* parce qu'elle est la question décisive à laquelle toutes les autres se rapportent de près ou de loin." (p. 19).

19. Rousseau, *Œuvres complètes,* p. 41.

20. Many references in *Rameau's Nephew* concern applause. They follow the Rousseauean view (expressed in *La Lettre à d'Alembert*) about applause being a sign of hypocrisy and moral self-indulgence. See, for example, p. 54: "Cet imbecile parterre les claque a tout rompre."

21. Diderot, *Le Neveu de Rameau,* pp. 84-85.

22. They could not, of course. *Le Neveu de Rameau* was not meant to be published in Diderot's lifetime. The text is a posthumous one. It was issued in circumstances which read like some of the more elaborate hoaxes of Diderot's own stories. The manuscript was first sent to St. Petersburg, later discovered on a Parisian bookstall, translated first into German and then into French. The authentic first edition of this work—first published edition of this work, that is—is not in French but in German. The *édition originale française* was a translation back into French of the earlier rendering of Goethe.

23. The most striking connection between these works concerns the similarity of the *homme orchestre* scene and the fantasy sequence of book two of *Le Rêve de d'Alembert* (the one where d'Alembert recounts his dream of *le marbre comestible* to Mlle de l'Espinasse and Dr. Bordeu).

24. This quotation comes from the opening page of *Candide.* "M. le baron était un des plus puissants seigneurs de la Westphalie, car son château avait une porte et des fenêtres."

25. For the philosophical background of this lesson, consult Ira Wade, *The Intellectual Development of Voltaire* (Princeton: Princeton Univ. Press, 1968).

26. Diderot, *Le Neveu de Rameau,* p. 84.

27. Stephen Heath, "Language, Literature, Materialism," *Substance,* XVII (1977), pp. 67-74.

28. Diderot, *Le Neveu de Rameau,* p. 83.

29. *Ibid.,* p. 86; p. 101.

30. The term comes from Peter Brook's study of the aesthetics of theater entitled *The Empty Space.* Brook distinguishes between four types of theater. They are deadly theater, holy theater, rough theater, and immediate theater. Classical French opera surely constitutes, in Lui's view at least, an example of lifeless or deadly theater. The art of the *homme orchestre* underscores the kind of holy theater spoken of by Brook.

31. Diderot, *Œuvres complètes,* (Assézat et Tourneaux) VII, 156.

32. The concept of "genetic" art is explored by Paul de Man in "Genesis and Genealogy in Nietzsche's *The Birth of Tragedy,*" *Diacritics,* II (Winter 1972), p. 48. For the concept of vegetable genius and related romantic concepts, see M. H. Abrams, *The Mirror and the Lamp* (New York: Norton, 1958). Another idea which bears study in this regard is the link between the virtuoso and the "monster." For this theme see Emita Hill, "Materialism and monsters in Diderot's *Le Rêve de d'Alembert,*" *Diderot Studies,* 10 (1968), pp. 67-93; and Jacques Proust, "Diderot et la philosophie du polype," *Revue des Sciences Humaines,* 182, pp. 21-30.

33. George May, *Le Dilemme du roman* (Paris: PUF, 1963).

34. The influence of Rousseau on *Rameau's Nephew* is discussed with great sensitivity by Donal O'Gorman, *Diderot the Satirist* (Toronto: Univ. of Toronto Press, 1971).

35. Jean Starobinski, *La Transparence et l'obstacle* (Paris: Gallimard, 1957).

36. A key feature of "dionysian" works is a shifting back and forth between silence and spoken language. See, for example, Walter F. Otto, *Dionysus, Myth and Cult* (Bloomington: Indiana Univ. Press, 1973). "However, there is nothing which reveals the supernatural meaning of the incredible noisemaking which announces the god and accompanies him so well as its counterpart of deathlike silence into which it suddenly changes. A wild uproar and a numbed silence—these are only different forms of the Nameless, of that which shatters all composure." (p. 93) The earlier quotation about "le jaillissement de la nature" comes from Georges Snyders, *Le Goût musical en France au XVIIe et XVIIIe siècle,* p. 110.

37. Rousseau uses *éloquence muette* in *La Lettre à d'Alembert* as a metaphor for sterile declamation. The phrase could also be turned inside out (or used satirically). As such, it would represent a true natural eloquence whose characteristics are silence and a kind of *mutisme.*

38. This term also comes from *La Lettre à d'Alembert* (the passage where Rousseau describes the falsehoods of classical theater). People applaud as a sign that they have been moved. In reality their clapping is a fiction, an act of vanity and illusion; and of as short a duration as the platitudes articulated on stage.

39. Diderot, *Le Neveu de Rameau,* p. 49.

Chapter IV: Anti-Theater

1. Jean Starobinski, *La Transparence et l'obstacle* (Paris: Gallimard, 1957). Derrida's concept of *supplémentarité* is surely related to strategies of irony first discussed in Starobinski's study.

2. Paul de Man, "The Rhetoric of Blindness: Jacques Derrida's Reading of Rousseau," in *Blindness and Insight* (New York: Oxford, 1971), pp. 102-41.

3. Rousseau, *Les Rêveries du promeneur solitaire,* ed. Marcel Raymond (Geneva: Droz, 1948).

4. Rousseau, *Œuvres complètes,* vol. I, ed. Pléiade (Paris: Gallimard, 1961), pp. 1046-47.

5. *Ibid.,* p. 1046.

6. Ronald Grimsley, *Jean-Jacques Rousseau* (Cardiff: Univ. of Wales, 1961), pp. 296-97.

7. Rousseau, *Œuvres complètes,* p. 1073. For the history of *le livre de la nature* see E. R. Curtius, *European Literature and the Latin Middle Ages* (New York: Harper, 1963). Other examples of such a text in eighteenth-century France include *Micromégas, Zadig,* and Diderot's *le grand rouleau (Jacques le fataliste).*

8. These are some of the plants Rousseau speaks of as forming his *herbier.* The *Flora Petrinsularis* is the encyclopedia of plant life found on the Isle de St. Pierre.

9. The references show a satirical side quite characteristic of Rousseau and point to the duality of lyricism and satire which informs many of his works.

10. Molière provides an example of traditional comedy (with the possible exception of *Le Misanthrope).* Examples of a more unresolved and "romantic" comedy can be found in Breton's *Anthologie de l'humour noir.* Among the authors Breton lists are Lewis Carroll, de Quincey, and Kafka.

11. Diderot, *Le Neveu de Rameau,* p. 87. The reversion to spoken French is a *coup de théâtre.* It creates a dramatic contrast or *alternance* between silence (or the "unsayable") and the all too colloquial idiom of French: the emblem, for Diderot's narrator, of repression and civilization.

12. *Ibid.,* p. 91.

13. *Ibid.*, p. 4.

14. This term was used by Paul de Man in his essay called "The Rhetoric of Temporality" in *Interpretation: Theory and Practice,* ed. Charles Singleton (Baltimore: Johns Hopkins, 1969).

15. Among many works of the time which underscore this procedure, one may single out *Le Jeu de l'amour et du hasard* and *Così fan tutte.*

16. Mikhail Bakhtin, *Rabelais and His World* (Cambridge: MIT, 1968), p. 40.

17. That this text does touch on madness can be seen by comparing it to the more controlled self-revelations of *Les Confessions.* Foucault makes much of the supposed madness of Rousseau and what he calls a "rhétorique de la folie."

18. Charles Baudelaire, *Œuvres complètes* (Paris: Gallimard, 1961), p. 987. The essential distinction in Baudelaire's essay is between "meaningful comedy" and "absolute comedy." Meaningful comedy takes society as its target. It is, he says, a uniquely French art: "En France, pays de pensée et de démonstration claires, où l'art vise naturellement et directement à l'utilité, le comique est généralement significatif." Absolute comedy portrays existence. Its subject is the fallen state of man and a split in consciousness. It does not result in laughter but in the kind of "satanic" reaction of "le sage" who "ne rit qu'en tremblant."

19. *Ibid.*, pp. 988-90.

20. Diderot, *Le Neveu de Rameau,* p. 5.

21. *Ibid.*, p. 19.

22. *Ibid.*, p. 5.

23. George Steiner, *Tolstoy or Dostoevsky* (New York: Vintage, 1959), p. 196.

24. Mikhail Bakhtin, *Rabelais and his World,* p. 166.

25. Diderot, *Le Neveu de Rameau,* p. 49; p. 57.

26. For this aspect see Stephen Werner, *Diderot's "Great Scroll": Narrative Art in Jacques le fataliste, Studies on Voltaire and the Eighteenth Century,* CXXVIII (1975), pp. 51-71.

27. The grotesque aspects of *La Religieuse* are discussed by Stephen Werner in "Diderot, Sade and the gothic novel," *Studies on Voltaire,* LXXIX (1971), pp. 79-92. The term "romantic agony" comes from Mario Praz, *The Romantic Agony* (Oxford: Oxford Univ. Press, 1951).

28. Diderot, *Le Neveu de Rameau,* p. 26.

29. *Ibid.,* p. 47.

30. *Ibid.,* p. 25.

31. *Ibid.,* p. 38.

32. Victor Fournel, *Les Rues du Vieux Paris* (Paris: Firmin-Didot, 1879), pp. 430-31.

33. *Ibid.*

34. For this subject see Jean Starobinski's article "Portrait de l'artiste en saltimbanque," *Critique,* XXV (December, 1969), pp. 1033-54.

35. The concept of cruelty finds especially keen expression in J. Kristeva's writings. See Julia Kristeva, *Semeiotike,* p. 161.

36. Jean Fabre's edition of *Le Neveu de Rameau* contains invaluable notes about cafés in the France of Diderot's time. The location of the Café de la Régence is discussed on p. 114. It was near the Palais Royal. Diderot's narrator also speaks of cafés as places where idlers (*fainéants*) waste their time "pushing wood" (p. 7). Here, too, a connection with Rousseau can be stressed. For Rousseau specifically refers to cafés in *La Lettre à d'Alembert*—his central meditation on *le spectacle* and modern culture—as a haven for loiterers and social malcontents.

37. *Beggar's Opera* is not, of course, to be taken as a specific literary influence on Diderot's text. Diderot did not know Gay's play (nor the latter *Rameau's Nephew*). Yet both writers share a common interest in what might be called "urban pastoral." The mode serves to dramatize a kind of trivialization of nature and myth.

38. William Empson, *Some Versions of Pastoral* (London: Chatto and Windus, 1935).

39. Jean Starobinski, "Dimensions imaginaires du XVIIIe siècle," *Les Lettres Nouvelles* (Nov.-Dec., 1964), p. 47.

40. "De maudites circonstances nous menent et nous menent fort mal" (p. 103). The image updates the concept of chance fundamental to carnival literature. Chance is to be taken in Diderot's text as cut off from the myth of *Fortuna*. What chance represents is *le hasard:* a random and fortuitous series of occurrences taking place without the order—and ultimately necessity—of myth.

Chapter V: *Satyre 2de*

1. Horace, *Satires, Epistles, and Ars Poetica*, p. 451.

2. Two studies may be singled out as being of special interest to an analysis of parody. They are the article by Yuri Tynianov (from which the quotations used in the text are drawn), "Destruction, Parodie," *Change,* II

(1969), pp. 67-76; and the recent study by Gérard Genette, *Palimpsestes: La Littérature au second degré* (Paris: Seuil, 1981). One can appreciate the special circumstances of parody by comparing it with pastiche (a term with which the former is often confused). Pastiches are brief. A given style or form is copied and shown to be vulnerable. It is, though, left intact. Parody, by contrast, is more of a transgressive mode. The art has a more complex temporal structure than pastiche as well. Parody seeks both to capture the essence of a given form and transform it: to break out of an allegiance to the past. The difference between parody and pastiche is illustrated by Proust. *Pastiches et mélanges* confirms the mode of pastiche. *A la recherche du temps perdu,* by contrast, shows the mark of parody: Proust's text has integrated the pastiche of the Goncourt brothers into a larger work which has transcended *le style artistique* (and the dandy consciousness which was rightly or wrongly associated with the Goncourt brothers).

3. Diderot, *Le Neveu de Rameau,* p. 96.

4. Jean Brun, *Socrates* (New York: Walker and Company, 1962), pp. 34-39.

5. Diderot, *Le Neveu de Rameau,* p. 98.

6. Peter Gay, *The Enlightenment: An Interpretation* (New York: Knopf, 1969), p. 102.

7. Arthur M. Wilson, *Diderot* (New York: Oxford, 1972), p. 109.

8. Jean Fabre, "Deux frères ennemis: Diderot et Jean-Jacques," *Diderot Studies,* III (1961), pp. 155-213.

9. Diderot, *Le Neveu de Rameau,* p. 80.

10. Georg Lukács, *The Young Hegel* (London: Merlin, 1973), p. 495.

11. G. W. F. Hegel, *The Phenomenology of Mind* (New York: Harper, 1967), pp. 509-91.

12. G. W. F. Hegel, *La Phénoménologie de l'Esprit* (Paris: Aubier, 1948).

13. Diderot, *Le Neveu de Rameau,* p. 83.

14. Lukács, *The Young Hegel,* p. 497.

15. Jacques's master is not put through Moi's initiation. He is a creature of pure fun: poking about in his pockets for his timepiece, taking pinches of snuff, and, in general, serving as an example of burlesque repetition. He repeats the philosophical formulae of Jacques, his seeming valet, but, in reality, philosophical mentor. The conversation, like so many chats in Diderot, is a parody of Socratic dialogue.

16. Lionel Trilling, *Beyond Culture* (New York: Viking, 1965). "There is ground for supposing that it *(Rameau's Nephew)* was known to Dostoevsky, whose *Notes from Underground* is a restatement of the essential idea of Diderot's dialogue in terms both more extreme and less genial. The Nephew is still on the defensive—he is naughtily telling secrets about the nature of man and society. Dostoevsky's underground man shouts aloud his envy and hatred and carries the ark of his self-hatred and alienation into a remorseless battle with what he calls the good and the beautiful, mounting an attack upon every belief not merely of bourgeois society but of the humanist tradition."

17. The superb *Bibliographie de Diderot* of Frederick Spears contains hundreds of articles on Diderot's life and the thematic interests that guide his work. Rare indeed, though, is the piece that studies Diderot's style. Several studies can be pointed to as essential to any inquiry into the question. They are: Leo Spitzer's *Linguistics and Literary History* (Princeton: Princeton Univ. Press, 1974); and Peter France's *Rhetoric and Truth in France* (Oxford: Clarendon, 1972), pp. 191-234. The last two pages of France's chapter deal with *Le Neveu de Rameau.*

18. The term carnival comes from Bakhtin's study of Rabelais *(Rabelais and his World)*. Carnival underscores a radical disjunction in the text. Through it, various influences or intertextualities are broken open and set to ferment. A clear definition of the procedure (one which stresses concerns of form as well as subject matter) can be found in a later study of Bakhtin: *Problems of Dostoevsky's Poetics,* pp. 100-16.

19. Jean Starobinski, "Le Philosophe, le géomètre, l'hybride," *Poétique,* XXI (1975). Goat-footed forms are, of course, emblematic of satire. For satire is inseparable from half-creatures (and satyrs).

20. Daniel Mornet, *Le Neveu de Rameau* (Paris: Editions Montcrestien, 1965), p. 120. Mornet specifically refers to Diderot's work as a novel.

21. The term "novelistic" comes from the English translation of René Girard's *Mensonge romantique et vérité romanesque.*

22. Gustave Lanson, *L'Art de la prose* (Paris: Arthème Fayard, 1907), p. 176.

23. For the menippean see Mikhail Bakhtin, *Rabelais and his World;* Northrop Frye, *Anatomy of Criticism;* and Julia Kristeva, *Semeiotike* (Paris: Seuil, 1969).

24. Northrop Frye, *Anatomy of Criticism,* p. 309. Kristeva defines the mode along similar lines: "La ménippée tient son nom du philosophe du IIIe siècle avant notre ère, Ménippe de Gadare (ses satires ne nous sont pas parvenues, nous connaissons leur existence par les témoignages de Diogène Laerce). Le terme fut employé par les Romains pour désigner un genre formé au Ier siècle avant n. e. (Varron: *Saturae menippeae).* Le genre apparaît pourtant beaucoup plus tôt: son premier représentant est peut-être Antisthène, élève de Socrate et l'un des auteurs du dialogue socratique. Héraclite a aussi écrit des ménippées (d'après Cicéron, il a créé un genre analogue dit *logistoricus).* Varron lui donna une stabilité déterminée. *L'Apocolocyntosis* de Sénèque en est un spécimen, aussi bien

que le *Satiricon* de Pétrone, les satires de Lucien, les *Métamorphoses* d'Ovide, le *Roman* d'Hippocrate...." (pp. 164-65).

25. The more recent studies of Kristeva seem especially marked by this tendency. See, for example, "La Musique parlée ou remarques sur la subjectivité dans la fiction, à propos du *Neveu de Rameau*," in *Langue et Langages de Leibnitz à l'Encyclopédie* (Paris: 10/18, 1977). She refers in this essay to *Rameau's Nephew* as a novel: "Ce roman est en effet un dialogue dans lequel l'autre ou la 2e personne se présente comme une 3e personne" (p. 163). One is indeed asked to read Diderot's work as a "musical novel" which anticipates Joyce: "Joyce, ou l'obstination *du Neveu de Rameau*," as she phrases it in the last line of the essay (p. 203).

26. Robert Scholes and Robert Kellogg, *The Nature of Narrative* (New York: Oxford, 1971), p. 107.

27. The American art critic Harold Rosenberg uses the phrase "the tradition of the new" to describe this phenomenon.

28. Georges Poulet, *Etudes sur le temps humain* (Edinburgh: Edinburgh Univ. Press, 1949), p. 202. Poulet speaks of "rétrécissement et expansion" as fundamental to the poetics of Rousseau. In *Shandyism, The Character of Romantic Irony* (Cambridge: Basil Blackwell, 1978), Peter Conrad makes a similar point: "Sterne revels in the formal paradox by arguing that the minutest philosophers are those with the most enlarged understandings. The smaller the inquiry, the larger its implications, and the greater the magnitude of soul it requires. As Jean Paul declared irony to be the sublime in miniature, so *contraction is the only way to expansion*" (p. 29).

29. Enharmonic means changing the name of a tone without changing its pitch (C sharp becoming D flat, for example). It can be thought of as a Socratic device, for it underscores a kind of critical freedom and play of form.

30. Diderot, *Le Neveu de Rameau*, p. 31.

31. George Steiner, *In Bluebeard's Castle* (New Haven: Yale Univ. Press, 1971), pp. 122-23.

Chapter VI: From Satire to Irony

1. Lilian R. Furst, *Fictions of Romantic Irony in European Narrative 1760-1857* (London: Macmillan Press, 1984), p. 24.

2. The mode is of course the "operatic" one discussed in the previous chapter. The distinction between satire and irony (and, in a general way, genre and mode) is touched on by André Jolles in *Formes simples* (Paris: Seuil, 1972), p. 203-04: "L'usage confond fréquemment la satire et l'ironie. Il n'y a là rien d'étonnant puisque certaines grandes œuvres de l'art commencent comme satire pour finir dans l'ironie: après s'être d'abord cru en face de l'objet de sa moquerie, après avoir espéré pouvoir le dénouer sans "compassion" l'auteur finit par voir à quel point il est proche de l'objet de sa moquerie, à quel point ses coups l'atteignent lui-même. On pense à Cervantes et à *Don Quichotte*. Dans d'autres œuvres les deux formes voisinent constamment et on a l'impression que le dénouement de l'Ironie et celui de la Satire se font la chasse: je pense à l'Arioste, à Rabelais et à tant de grands romantiques allemands."

3. Peter Conrad, *Shandyism: The Character of Romantic Irony* (New York: Harper & Row, 1978), p. 169.

4. Friedrich Schlegel, *Kritische Schriften* (Munich: Carl Hanser Verlag, 1964), p. 510. Schlegel's essay also emphasizes the connection between modern or ironic narratives and the Socratic dialogue: "Die Romane sind die sokratischen Dialoge unserer zeit." An excellent bibliography of the subject (in French, English, and German) can be found in Furst's *Fictions of Romantic Irony,* pp. 261-63. See also D. C. Muecke, *The Compass of Irony* (London: Methuen, 1969); René Bourgeois, *L'Ironie romantique* (Grenoble: Presses Universitaires de Grenoble, 1974); and Ingrid Strohschneider-Kohrs, *Die romantische Ironie in Theorie und Gestaltung* (Tübingen: Niemeyer, 1977).

5. Ph. Lacoue-Labarthe and J.-L. Nancy provide the following analysis of *Witz* in *L'Absolu littéraire* (Paris: Seuil, 1978): "'mot d'esprit,' voire 'jeu de mots,' et aussi faculté d'en produire, et plus largement d'inventer une combinaison de choses hétérogènes, reste comme on le sait intraduisible."

6. Furst, p. 24. For the rhetoric of Socratic irony and its claims on the aesthetics of modernity, see Hegel's *Lectures on the Philosophy of Religion,* and three studies of Kierkegaard. They are: *Philosophical Fragments; Concluding Unscientific Postscript;* and the work which first established the connection between Socrates and modernity: *The Concept of Irony.* Kierkegaard defines Socratic irony as "infinite absolute negativity": "It is negativity because it only negates; it is infinite because it negates not this or that phenomenon; and it is absolute because it negates by virtue of a higher which is not. Irony establishes nothing, for that which is to be established lies behind it. It is a divine madness which rages like a Tamerlane and leaves not one stone standing upon another in its wake." *The Concept of Irony* (Bloomington: Indiana Univ. Press, 1961), p. 278.

7. For *Rameau's Nephew* as a satire of social parasitism see the lively study by J. F. Falvey, *Le Neveu de Rameau* (London: Grant and Cutler, 1985).

8. Cyril Connolly, *The Modern Movement* (London: Deutsch and Hamilton, 1965).

9. Ernst Curtius, *European Literature and the Latin Middle Ages* (New York: Harper, 1963). The last section of this book deals with what Curtius calls "modern canon formation." Another key contribution to the subject is the essay by Paul de Man on "Literary History and Literary Modernity," *(Blindness and Insight):* "It is perhaps somewhat disconcerting to learn that our usage of the word goes back to the late fifth century of our era and that there is nothing modern about the concept of modernity. It is even more disturbing to discover the host of complications that beset one as soon as a conceptual definition of the term is attempted, especially with regard to literature. One is soon forced to resort to paradoxical

formulations, such as defining the modernity of a literary period as the manner in which it discovers the impossibility of being modern." (p. 144)

10. For the theme of the modern seen against the special interests of the eighteenth century and the battle of "les anciens et les modernes," see Werner Krauss, "Cartaud de la Villate und die Entstehung des geschichtlichen Weltbildes in der Frühaufklärung," *Studien zur Deutschen und Französischen Aufklärung* (Berlin: 1963); and H. R. Jauss's introduction to his edition of Charles Perrault, *Parallèle des Anciens et des Modernes* (Munich, 1964). Another article of interest is the entry by Jauss entitled "Antique/moderne (querelle des Anciens et des Modernes)," in the *Historisches Wörterbuch der Philosophie,* ed. Joachim Ritter (Basel: Schwabe, 1971), pp. 409-10.

11. For anxiety and the related theme of belatedness, see Harold Bloom, *The Anxiety of Influence* (New York: Oxford, 1973).

12. Paul de Man, *Blindness and Insight,* p. 149.

13. A nice discussion of the concept appears in the spirited essay by Cyrus Hamlin, "Platonic Dialogue and Romantic Irony: Prolegomenon to a Theory of Literary Narrative," *Canadian Review of Comparative Literature* (Winter 1976), pp. 5-26.

14. Walter Benjamin, *The Origin of German Tragic Drama* (London: New Left Books, 1977), p. 44.

15. The quotation is from *Jacques le fataliste.* See Diderot, *Œuvres romanesques* (Paris: Garnier, 1962), p. 545.

Bibliography

Abrams, M. H. *The Mirror and the Lamp: Romantic Theory and the Critical Tradition.* New York: Norton, 1958.

──────. *Natural Supernaturalism.* New York: Norton, 1973.

Adams, D. J. *Diderot, Dialogue and Debate.* Liverpool: Francis Cairns, 1986.

──────. "*Le Neveu de Rameau* since 1950." *Studies on Voltaire and the Eighteenth Century,* 217 (1983), pp. 371-87.

Bakhtin, Mikhail. *Problems of Dostoevsky's Poetics.* Ann Arbor: Ardis, 1973.

──────. *Rabelais and His World.* Cambridge: MIT, 1968.

Balcou, Jean. "La Poésie de la satire dans *Le Neveu de Rameau.*" In *Approches des Lumières: Mélanges offerts à Jean Fabre.* Paris: Klincksieck, 1974, pp. 17-29.

Bardez, Jean Michel. *Diderot et la Musique.* Paris: Champion, 1975.

Barricelli, Jean-Pierre. "Music and the structure of Diderot's *Le Neveu de Rameau.*" *Criticism,* 5 (1963), pp. 95-111.

Barzun, Jacques. "The Mystery in *Rameau's Nephew.*" *Diderot Studies,* XVII (1973), pp. 109-16.

Bate, W. Jackson. *The Burden of the Past and the English Poet.* New York: Norton, 1970.

Baud-Bovy, Samuel. "Rousseau as a Musician." *TLS,* 20 July 1973, pp. 829-30.

Baudelaire, Charles. *Œuvres complètes.* Paris: Gallimard, 1966.

Behler, E. *Klassische Ironie, romantische Ironie, tragische Ironie. Zum Ursprung dieser Begriffe.* Darmstadt, 1972.

Benjamin, Walter. *Der Begriff der Kunstkritik in der Deutschen Romantik.* Frankfurt am Main: Suhrkamp, 1973.

——————. *The Origins of German Tragic Drama.* London: New Left Books, 1977.

Blum, Carol. *Diderot: The Virtue of a Philosopher.* New York: Viking, 1974.

Bourgeois, René. *L'Ironie romantique.* Grenoble, 1974.

Bremner, Geoffrey. "Contradictions in Diderot's scientific philosophy and *Le Neveu de Rameau.*" *French Studies,* XXXIV (1980), pp. 153-67.

——————. *Order and Chance: The Pattern of Diderot's Thought.* Cambridge: Cambridge Univ. Press, 1983.

Brook, Peter. *The Empty Stage.* New York: Atheneum, 1968.

Brooks, Peter. *The Melodramatic Imagination.* New Haven: Yale Univ. Press, 1976.

Brun, Jean. *Socrate.* Paris: PUF, 1960.

Chouillet, Anne-Marie. *Denis Diderot, Colloque International.* Paris: Aux Amateurs de Livres, 1985.

Chouillet, Jacques. *Diderot.* Paris: SEDES, 1977.

———. "L'Espace urbain et sa fonction textuelle dans *Le Neveu de Rameau.*" *La Ville au XVIIIe siècle.* Aix-en-Provence: ADISUD, 1975, pp. 71-81.

———. *La Formation des idées esthétiques de Diderot.* Paris: A. Colin, 1973.

Coffey, Michael. *Roman Satire.* London: Methuen, 1977.

Cohen, Huguette. "La tradition gauloise et le carnavalesque." *Denis Diderot, Colloque International.* Paris: Aux Amateurs de Livres, 1985.

Coleman, Patrick. *Rousseau's Political Imagination: Rule and Representation in La Lettre à d'Alembert.* Geneva: Droz, 1984.

Conrad, Peter. *Romantic Opera and Literary Form.* Berkeley: Univ. of California Press, 1977.

———. *Shandyism: The Character of Romantic Irony.* Cambridge: Blackwell, 1978.

Couty, Daniel. *Le Neveu de Rameau: profil d'une œuvre.* Paris, 1972.

Creech, James. "*Le Neveu de Rameau:* the diary of a reading." *Modern Language Notes,* XCV (1980), pp. 995-1004.

Crocker, Lester. *Diderot's Chaotic Order.* Princeton: PUP, 1974.

Curtius, Ernst Robert. *European Literature and the Latin Middle Ages.* New York: Harper, 1963.

Desné, Roland. *Diderot et le Neveu de Rameau: Essai d'Explication.* Paris: Centre d'Etudes et de Recherches Marxistes, n. d.

——————. "Le Neveu de Rameau dans l'ombre et la lumière du XVIIIe siècle." *Studies in Voltaire and the Eighteenth Century,* XXV (1963), pp. 493-507.

Dieckmann, Herbert. *Cinq Leçons sur Diderot.* Geneva: Droz, 1959.

——————. "Diderot's Conception of Genius." *Journal of the History of Ideas,* 2 (1941), pp. 151-82.

——————. "The Relationship between Diderot's Satire I and Satire II." *Romanic Review,* XLIII (1952), pp. 12-26.

Dieckmann, Jane Marsh. "A Zerbina penserete: a Note on Diderot's Epigraph." In *Studies in Eighteenth Century French Literature presented to Robert Niklaus.* Ed. J. H. Fox. Exeter: Univ. of Exeter, 1975.

Doolittle, James. *Rameau's Nephew: A Study of Diderot's Second Satire.* Geneva: Droz, 1960.

Duchet, Michèle and Michel Launay. *Entretiens sur Le Neveu de Rameau.* Paris: Nizet, 1967.

Elliott, R. C. "Saturnalia, Satire, and Utopia." *The Yale Review,* NS 55 (1965/66), pp. 521-36.

Fabre, Jean. "Deux frères ennemis: Diderot et Jean-Jacques." *Diderot Studies,* 3 (1961), pp. 155-213.

Falvey, J. F. *Le Neveu de Rameau.* London: Grant and Cutler, 1985.

Fanger, Donald. *Dostoevsky and Romantic Realism.* Chicago: Univ. of Chicago Press, 1974.

Feinbert, L. "Satire: The Inadequacy of Recent Definitions." *Genre,* I (1968), pp. 31-37.

Fellows, Otis. *Diderot.* New York: Twayne, 1977.

——————. "The Theme of Genius in Diderot's *Neveu de Rameau.*" *Diderot Studies,* II (1952), pp. 168-99.

Fontenay, Elisabeth de. *Diderot ou le matérialisme enchanté.* Paris: Grasset, 1981.

Fournel, Victor. *Les Rues du Vieux Paris.* Paris: Firmin-Didot, 1879.

France, Peter. *Diderot.* Oxford: OUP, 1983.

——————. *Rhetoric and Truth in France: Descartes to Diderot.* Oxford: Clarendon, 1972.

Frazer, James. *The New Golden Bough.* New York: Doubleday, 1961.

Fried, Michael. *Absorption and Theatricality: Painting and the Beholder in the Age of Diderot.* Berkeley: Univ. of California Press, 1980.

Furst, Lilian R. *Fictions of Romantic Irony in European Narrative, 1760-1857.* London: Macmillan Press, 1984.

Frye, Northrop. *Anatomy of Criticism.* Princeton: Princeton Univ. Press, 1957.

——————. "The Nature of Satire." *University of Toronto Quarterly,* XIV (Oct. 1944), pp. 75-89.

Gans, Eric. *Musset et le drame tragique.* Paris: Corti, 1974.

Gay, Peter. *The Enlightenment: An Intepretation.* New York: Knopf, 1966.

Genette, Gérard. *Palimpsestes: la littérature au second degré.* Paris: Seuil, 1980.

Gilman, Margaret. *The Idea of Poetry in France from Houdar de la Motte to Baudelaire.* Cambridge: Harvard Univ. Press, 1958.

Girard, René. *Mensonge romantique et vérité romanesque.* Paris: Grasset, 1961.

Gossman, Lionel. *French Society and Culture: Background for Eighteenth-Century Literature.* Englewood Cliffs, N.J.: Prentice-Hall, 1972.

Grimsley, Ronald. *Jean-Jacques Rousseau.* Cardiff: Univ. of Wales Press, 1961.

Guiragossian, Diana. *Voltaire's Facéties.* Geneva: Droz, 1963.

Hamlin, Cyrus. "Platonic Dialogue and Romantic Irony: Prolegomenon to a Theory of Literary Narrative." *Canadian Review of Comparative Literature,* III (Winter 1976), pp. 5-26.

Hantsch, Ingrid. "Bibliographie zur Gattungspoetik (2): Theorie des Satire (1900-1971)." *Zeitschrift für Französische Sprache und Literatur,* LXXXII (1972), pp. 153-56.

Hayman, David. "Au-delà de Bakhtine." *Poétique,* XIII (1973), pp. 76-94.

Heath, Stephen. "Language, Literature, Materialism." *Sub-Stance,* XVII (1977), pp. 67-74.

―――. "Théâtre du langage." *Critique,* 331 (Dec. 1974), pp. 1053-81.

Hegel, G. W. F. *La Phénoménologie de l'Esprit.* Paris: Aubier, 1939.

Hobson, Marion. *The Object of Art: The Theory of Illusion in Eighteenth-Century France.* Cambridge: CUP, 1982.

Hyppolite, Jean. *Etudes sur Marx et Hegel.* Paris: Rivière, 1955.

——————. *Genèse et Structure de la Phénoménologie de l'Esprit de Hegel.* Paris: Aubier Montaigne, 1946.

Jack, Ian. *Augustan Satire.* Oxford: Clarendon, 1952.

Jauss, H. R. *Nachahmung und Illusion.* Munich: Fink, 1969.

Jeanmaire, H. *Dionysos.* Paris: Payot, 1970.

Jenny, Laurent. "Le discours du carnaval." *Littérature,* XVI (Dec. 1974), pp. 19-36.

Josephs, Herbert. *Diderot's Dialogue of Language and Gesture.* Columbus: Ohio State Univ. Press, 1969.

Jolliffe, J. W. "Satyre: Satura: SATYRA: A Study in Confusion." *Bibliothèque d'Humanisme et Renaissance,* 18 (1956), pp. 84-95.

Kaplan, James. "Notes on *Le Neveu de Rameau.*" *Romance Notes,* XXI (1979), pp. 68-74.

Kayser, Wolfgang. *The Grotesque in Art and Literature.* New York: Columbia, 1981.

Kierkegaard, Soren. *The Concept of Irony.* Bloomington: Indiana Univ. Press, 1968.

Kristeva, Julia. "La Musique parlée ou remarques sur la subjectivité dans la fiction, à propos du *Neveu de Rameau.*" In *Langue et Langages de Leibnitz à l'Encyclopédie.* Ed. M. Duchet and M. Jalley. Paris: 10/18, 1977.

———. *Semeiotike*. Paris: Seuil, 1969.

Lanson, Gustave. *L'Art de la prose*. Paris: Arthème Fayard, 1907.

Laufer, Roger. "Structure et signification du *Neveu de Rameau*." *Revue des Sciences Humaines*, 25 (1960), pp. 399-413.

Launay, Michel. "Etude du *Neveu de Rameau:* hypothèse pour une recherche collective." *La Pensée*, 118 (Dec. 1964), pp. 85-92.

Lewinter, Roger. *Diderot ou les mots de l'absence*. Paris: Editions Champ Libre, 1976.

Loy, J. Robert. "Diderot's meditated *plan d'un opéra comique*." *Romanic Review*, 46 (1955), pp. 3-24.

Lukács, Georg. *Theorie des Romans*. Berlin: Cassirer, 1920.

———. *The Young Hegel*. London: Merlin Press, 1973.

de Man, Paul. *Blindness and Insight*. New York: Oxford, 1971.

———. "The Rhetoric of Temporality." In *Interpretation: Theory and Practice*. Ed. Charles Singleton. Baltimore: Johns Hopkins, 1969, pp. 173-209.

Marmier, Jean. *Horace en France au 17e siècle*. Paris: PUF, 1962.

Mason, H. T. *Pierre Bayle and Voltaire*. London: Oxford Univ. Press, 1963.

Mason, John Hope. *The Irresistible Diderot*. London: Quartet Books, 1982.

Maurer, Karl. "Die Satire in der Weise des Horaz als Kunstform von Diderots *Neveu de Rameau*." *Romanische Forschungen*, LXIV (1952), pp. 365-404.

Mauzi, Robert. *L'Idée du bonheur dans la littérature et la pensée françaises au XVIIIe siècle.* Paris: Colin, 1960.

May, Georges. "L'Angoisse de l'échec et la genèse du *Neveu de Rameau.*" *Diderot Studies,* III (1961), pp. 285-308.

──────. *Le Dilemme du roman au XVIIIe siècle.* Paris: PUF, 1963.

May, Gita. *Diderot et Baudelaire: critiques d'art.* Geneva: Droz, 1957.

Meyer, Paul H. "The Unity and Structure of Diderot's *Neveu de Rameau.*" *Criticism,* II (1959-60), pp. 362-86.

Molbjerg, Hans. *Aspects de l'esthétique de Diderot.* Copenhagen: J. H. Schultz, 1964.

Mornet, Daniel. *Le Neveu de Rameau.* Paris: Ed. Montchrestier, 1965.

Mortier, Roland. "L'Original selon Diderot." *Saggi e Ricerche di Letteratura Francese,* LV (1963), pp. 141-57.

Muecke, D. C. *The Compass of Irony.* London: Methuen, 1969.

Nancy, Jean-Luc. *L'Absolu littéraire.* Paris: Seuil, 1978.

Nietzsche, F. *The Birth of Tragedy and the Genealogy of Morals.* New York: Doubleday Anchor, 1956.

Niklaus, Robert. *A Literary History of France: The Eighteenth Century, 1715-1789.* London: Benn, 1970.

O'Gorman, Donal. *Diderot the Satirist: Le Neveu de Rameau and Related Works.* Toronto: Univ. of Toronto Press, 1971.

──────. "Myth and Metaphor in *Rameau's Nephew.*" *Diderot Studies,* XVII (1973), pp. 117-30.

Otto, Walter F. *Dionysus, Myth and Cult*. Bloomington: Indiana Univ. Press, 1973.

Pfister, Manfred. "Bibliographie zur Gattungspoetik." *Zeitschrift für Französische Sprache,* LXXXIII (1973), pp. 240-54.

Pomeau, René. *Diderot, sa vie, son œuvre*. Paris: PUF, 1967.

―――――. "Sur une étude structurale du *Neveu de Rameau.*" *RHLF,* LXXVIII (1978), pp. 449-53.

Poulet, Georges. *Etudes sur le temps humain*. Paris: Plon, 1950.

Praz, Mario. *The Romantic Agony*. Oxford: Oxford Univ. Press, 1951.

Proust, Jacques. "A propos d'un plan d'opéra-comique de Diderot." *Revue d'Histoire du Théâtre,* VII (1955), pp. 173-88.

―――――. "De l'*Encyclopédie* au *Neveu de Rameau:* l'objet et le texte." In *Recherches nouvelles sur quelques écrivains des Lumières*. Geneva: Droz, 1972.

Rex, W. E. "Two Scenes from *Le Neveu de Rameau.*" *Diderot Studies,* XX, pp. 245-66.

Riddel, Joseph. "Pound and the Decentered Image." *The Georgia Review,* XXIX (Fall 1975), pp. 565-626.

Riffaterre, Michel. *Essais de stylistique structurale*. Paris: Flammarion, 1971.

Robert, Marthe. *The Old and the New*. Berkeley: Univ. of California Press, 1977.

Robrieux, Jean-Jacques. "Jean-Philippe Rameau et l'opinion philosophique en France au dix-huitième siècle." *Studies on Voltaire and the Eighteenth Century,* 238 (1985), pp. 273-395.

Roger, Jacques. *Les Sciences de la vie dans la pensée française du XVIIIe siècle.* Paris: Colin, 1963.

Rosenkranz, Karl. *Diderots Leben und Werke.* Leipsig: Brockhaus, 1866.

Rousseau, Jean-Jacques. *Œuvres complètes,* ed. Pléiade. Paris: Gallimard, 4 vols.

—————. *Les Rêveries du promeneur solitaire.* ed. Marcel Raymond. Lille: Girard, 1948.

Rousset, Jean. *Narcisse Romancier.* Paris: Corti, 1973.

—————. "Qu'est-ce que le talent du comédien?" *Annales Jean-Jacques Rousseau,* XXXVII (1966-68), pp. 19-34.

Rudd, Niall. *The Satires of Horace.* Cambridge: Cambridge Univ. Press, 1966.

Scheler, Max. *L'Homme de Ressentiment.* Paris: Gallimard, 1970.

Scholes, Robert, and R. Kellog. *The Nature of Narrative.* New York: Oxford, 1966.

Schonert, Jorg. *Roman und Satire im 18. Jahrhundert.* Stuttgart: J. B. Metzlersche, 1969.

Seguin, Pierre. *Diderot: le discours et les choses.* Paris: Klincksieck, 1978.

Seznec, Jean. "Diderot and Neo-classicism." *The Listener,* (Oct. 26, 1972), pp. 535-37.

―――――. *Essais sur Diderot et l'Antiquité.* Oxford: Clarendon, 1957.

―――――. *The Survival of the Pagan Gods.* New York: Harper, 1961.

Sherman, Carol. *Diderot and the Art of the Dialogue.* Geneva: Droz, 1976.

Smith, Patrick J. *A Historical Study of the Opera Libretto.* New York: Schirmer, 1970.

Snyders, Georges. *Le Goût musical en France au XVIIe et XVIIIe siècles.* Paris: Vrin, 1968.

Souviron, Marie. *Le Malheur d'un vicieux, dialogue socratique: hypothèse de lecture pour Le Neveu de Rameau.* Paris: Centre d'Etudes et de Recherches Marxistes, 1972.

Spears, Frederick. *Bibliographie de Diderot.* Geneva: Droz, 1980.

Spitzer, Leo. *Linguistics and Literary History.* Princeton: Princeton Univ. Press, 1974.

Starobinski, Jean. "*Candide* et la question de l'autorité." In *Essays on the age of Enlightenment in honor of Ira O. Wade.* Geneva: Droz, 1977, pp. 305-12.

―――――. "Diderot et la parole des autres." *Critique,* (Jan. 1972), pp. 3-22.

―――――. "Dimensions imaginaires du XVIIIe siècle." *Les Lettres nouvelles,* (Nov.-Dec., 1964), pp. 47-63.

―――――. "Le Dîner chez Bertin." In *Das Komische.* Ed. W. Preisendanz and R. Warning. Munich: W. Fink, 1976, pp. 191-204.

―――――. "L'incipit du *Neveu de Rameau.*" NRF, 347 (1981), pp. 42-64.

―――――. "Le Philosophe, le géomètre, l'hybride." *Poétique,* XXI (1975), pp. 8-23.

―――――. "Portrait de l'artiste en Saltimbanque." *Critique,* XXV (Dec., 1969), pp. 1033-54.

―――――. *Jean-Jacques Rousseau. La Transparence et l'obstacle.* Paris: Gallimard, 1957.

Steiner, George. *In Bluebeard's Castle.* New Haven: Yale Univ. Press, 1971.

―――――. *Tolstoy or Dostoevsky.* New York: Knopf, 1961.

Strohschneider-Kohrs, I. *Die romantische Ironie in Theorie und Gestaltung.* Tübingen, 1960.

Sullivan, J. P. *Satire: Critical Essays on Roman Literature.* Bloomington: Indiana Univ. Press, 1963.

Sumi, Yoichi. *Le Neveu de Rameau: Caprices et logiques du jeu.* Tokyo: France Tosho, 1975.

―――――. "Autour de l'image du jeu d'échecs chez l'auteur du *Neveu de Rameau.*" In *Recherches nouvelles sur quelques écrivains des Lumières,* ed. Jacques Proust. Geneva: Droz, 1972, pp. 341-63.

Szondi, Peter. *Theorie des modernen Dramas.* Frankfurt-am-Main: Suhrkampf, 1968.

Thomas, R. G. "Chess as a metaphor in *Le Neveu de Rameau.*" *Forum for Modern Language Studies,* XVIII (1982), pp. 63-74.

Tillich, Paul. *Das Dämonische.* Tübingen: J. C. B. Mohr, 1926.

Trilling, Lionel. *Beyond Culture.* New York: Viking Press, 1965.

───────. *Sincerity and Authenticity.* Cambridge: Harvard Univ. Press, 1972.

Trousson, Raymond. *Socrate devant Voltaire, Diderot et Rousseau.* Paris: Minard, 1967.

Tynianov, Yuri. "Destruction, parodie." *Change,* II (1969), pp. 67-76.

Ullman, B. L. "Satura and Satire." *Classical Philology,* 8 (1913), pp. 172-94.

Undank, Jack. *Diderot.* Madison: Coda Press, 1979.

Vartanian, Aram. "Trembley's polyp, La Mettrie, and eighteenth-century French materialism." *Journal of the History of Ideas,* 11 (1950), pp. 259-86.

Wade, Ira. *The Intellectual Development of Voltaire.* Princeton: Princeton Univ. Press, 1968.

Werner, Stephen. *Diderot's "Great Scroll": Narrative Art in Jacques le fataliste. Studies on Voltaire and the Eighteenth Century,* CXXVIII (1975).

───────. "Diderot: Les Derniers Ecrits." In *Diderot, Les Dernières Années,* ed. Peter France and Anthony Strugnell. Edinburgh: EUP, 1985, pp. 171-79.

───────. "Irony and the essay: Diderot's 'Regrets sur ma vieille robe de chambre.' " In *Diderot: Digression and Dispersion,* ed. Jack Undank and Herbert Josephs. Lexington: French Forum, 1984, pp. 269-77.

Wills, Gary. "Diderot." *New York Review of Books,* Sept. 18, 1975.

Wilson, Arthur. *Diderot* New York: Oxford, 1972.

Zuber, Roger. "La Satire." *Encyclopaedia Universalis*. Paris: Encyclopaedia Universalis, 1968, XIV, p. 691.